Prisonegg

poems by

Jonathan Pessant

Finishing Line Press
Georgetown, Kentucky

Prisonegg

ACKNOWLEDGMENTS

As Safe As One Can Get In A Marriage, *Pedestal Magazine*
Crush & Feel, *Collateral Journal*
combat:peace, *Stonecoast Review*
Synthetic Cow's Milk, *Warm Milk Publishing*
The Impermanence of Being Alone, *Goose River Anthology*
Uncle Sam, Milltown Press, *G.I. Days: An Anthology of Military Life*
Vaporware, *Tokyo Poetry Journal, Issue 14: EROS*
Stomp and Drag, Military Experience & Arts, As You Were: *The Military
Review*
The War Chip, Middle West Press, *Giant Robot Poems Anthology Vol. 1*

"Prison" and "Egg" definitions were found online @ *Merriam-Webster*

Special thanks to the Post 9/11 GI Bill

Publisher: Leah Huete de Maines
Editor: Christen Kincaid
Cover Art: Samantha Couste
Author Photo: Jonathan Pessant
Cover Design: Elizabeth Maines McCleavy

Order online: www.finishinglinepress.com
also available on amazon.com

Author inquiries and mail orders:
Finishing Line Press
PO Box 1626
Georgetown, Kentucky 40324
USA

Contents

prison // **egg**
a place or situation from which you cannot escape
*
an animal reproductive body consisting of an ovum
together with its nutritive and protective envelopes
and having the capacity to develop into a new
individual capable of independent existence

How Not to Write a Military Prison Poem
after Bruce Lack

Never enter.
Never sign the contract.
Your blood is far too valuable
for it to soak into the clean
white emptiness of paper.

When the recruiter lies believe him, when
he shares a war story, believe him. As he shakes
your hand and pats you on the back believe
the lies, the encouragement he offers.
As he smiles you out the door, believe the last lie:
You'll be fine.

Never believe the man who is eager
for a strip search, a man who's eager
to bend over, spread his cheeks, pull
back his foreskin, open his mouth,
move his tongue around.
He does this because he's a liar.

If you want to believe in something
believe the prison-fist in your face,
believe the blood-spit on your shined boots,
believe the cut wrists that look like
hamburger on top of human steak.

Lie to yourself.
When the bottle's empty
lie to yourself.
When you remember how you blacked out
remember how you blacked out
for the next night's blackout.

There's no metaphor for confinement.
When you walk through the gate
you start to suffocate.

Test Pit

You stood there, that one tooth always grinning beyond your
clenched lips. That non-smile bit into me.
      I wasn't part of the laughter at the gravel pit, granite
being crushed so fine it erased
          all history of where in the stratification it belonged.
          I wasn't part of your heritage, of a wholly male history.
          I was unmale to you.

Yeah, I didn't like trucks. I sure wasn't gonna be part of the family
construction business.
I couldn't tell you
          where a distributor cap went
          what percentage of oil and gas to mix
          how to change a spark plug
          why diesel was different from leaded
          or who the hell this Uncle Henry you kept talking about
          every goddamn weekend.

That stuff didn't bother me though, not really.
 Not really until I was older
did I realize I thought you despised me. Maybe you did. Don't
know. I care
          and worry
          and wonder
          and yearn
          only after you died and gave away everything to your
          second wife and her family.
          You were weak for not knowing how to live with yourself.
          You deserve her. That's what you get, to live and die a
          thousand times
          in my fantasies. In your will there'd be nothing for me; I'd
          be crushed.
          You gave away our ancestral land, and the house I ran to
          as a child,
          to a stranger who drives by every day. Waves to me like
          I'm the asshole.

I grew up so I could be the disappointment
        not winning baseball, football, even foosball,
        losing summer afternoon wrestling matches,
        a dozen cousins not caring I wasn't the man I needed
        to be
        victorious, pointing fingers in faces and laughing.

I was the first one to attend college. Of all your
grandchildren, I was the one.
Why hadn't you and Grammie come to my graduation?
Years later your daughter told me you and Grammie were
half way
to campus, but turned the truck around. No further
comment. Just red-faced.

                Yeah, I'll show you
                I'm a man.

The Army recruiting office was in a strip mall, in a small
office full of flags and bullshit.
I remember the B&W photo of you, standing on the steps of
city hall, waiting with the other recruits.
        You looked like a thug, like doughboy death.
        The photo remains
        in my possession,
        you're still a ghost pressed flat.

You never did shake my hand
for being the only one of my cousins to serve.
Patriotic? Nah! Just paying back my college loans.
                I spent 7 years looking
                at balls and dicks and assholes
                in prison, where my fellow
                guards were as guilty
                as the inmates. The history
                of rocks and how rocks
                behave under pressure.

When I got married, you did not attend.
Was it because she was Black,
or that you were so flabbergasted
I wasn't gay?
I'd hate to think of either option as an opportunity to disappoint.

When I was little, Grammie sat me down at the kitchen table full
of photos; history like food.
Each one left residue, left hunger. We'd place them into stories,
laugh and cry and feel warm, but
you'd come in wanting lunch, hands engine-greased. Lava soap
scrapping away the stories
you told my male cousins. You'd grunt-laugh without me. In the
garage not meant for me.

You'd always call me Charlie. I thought it was some war thing,
some way to say I was the enemy.
Didn't know it was your name too

                              until it was too late to worry
                              about the double-edgedness
                              it compressed upon us both.

            Did I frighten you?
            Was I too close, did you want to be me?
            I frighten myself sometimes,
            wonder if our crushed rocks
            are enough
            to line a cemetery.

You only ever asked me one question.
            No   I won't make any money as an archaeologist.

The War Chip

plug it in and go
kill humans
and robots
and those
earmarked enemies.

let the war
chip crush
brains and
rust meat
like metal.

when life leaves
take it out and
jam the program
into other
obscene machines,

into those
who haven't
lost use of their
carbon-fiber
trigger fingers,

whose hearts
haven't yet thumped
against spent
shells yet.
life's forced out

circuit veins.
spark, spurt.
bodies like
cobalt rivers,
evaporate.

Prisonegg

In the middle of fly-over country, atop a ridge running parallel
to a slow-moving mucky river, within the false security of stone,
mortar, and ancient brick ramparts, and down below where
the boilers heat the floors, where inmates are drugged, are
handcuffed daily, and are occasionally removed forcibly from
their cells, four military guards laugh as an egg fries on the
winter-grey painted cement floor. The twelfth day of their last
twelve-hour midnight shift nears, sweat in their brown t-shirts
dries rings of white around their necks, under their arms. They
are past delirium, more akin to silt from compressed brick.

> Sleep comes in summer
> for these men, for these men hang
> their dreams in winter.

We live on the second floor of a bomb shelter, and out the
window, across the street, looming brick by brick and blotting
out both dawn and dusk, is a prison. Behind, the evening sun
hangs on the horizon, pulling the last sweltering moments from
the day; at sunset sirens sing like nursery rhymes. Is it a tornado,
or a bomb? No matter, we always go outside to look. Through the
night, politicians and generals amend battle plans. And when the
morning sun creeps back, waking those on guard duty, waking
those souls in prison but not behind bars, we wish it had been the
bomb and not the tornado.

> Blowing past the rain
> the bough breaks, the leaf is just
> as red in July.

The 2002 video is full of grainy pride. Violence exasperates the air, no one breaths. In the prison control room, three guards clench their hands like grenades; a fourth sits back, observing. They play the YouTube video for a seventh time. *Let the bodies hit the floor* blasts out from the computer speaker, *nothing wrong with me*. A bird's eye view of justifications, the pilot's commentary, distant and surgical. But in the control room, voices say *fucking sand nigger* and *get that towelhead*. The fourth soldier gags, gags like Alex on stage reaching for tits. He dry heaves till a broken nose feels better than state sanctioned porno.

> Prisoneggs neatly
> held hostage in a soft flat
> summer tornado.

Shock n Awe,
or we share the same insanity,
or the horror of meeting your future

wife's family. Who will see me
as a son
or brother
or a good fit
into their Sunday afternoon.

After church. Grandma's house.
Stouffers mac n cheese, deep fried
chicken, country-style breasts and drums
(what your niece calls chicken on the big bone)
collard greens with soft burnt bacon
cornbread—too sweet—and a couple
Bisquick biscuits dropped
from an ice cream scoop onto a small hot pan,
just for the new man in your life. I haven't
given up my New England for your Midwest yet,
but I'm trying

for the first time. Your little niece calls me
brother man, grabs my hand, doesn't
let go, asks me questions no other person would
get the answers to.
Marriage?
Kids?
Wedding day?
Happy?
Aren't you?
A shelling every Sunday
too honest to lie to.

Every weekend we'd escape from prison,
from Leavenworth to KCMO
from one confinement to another,
following the muddy Missouri.

Sometimes the silt of constant travel
erodes the banks of a relationship.

Sometimes I'd hem and haw
and be grumpy till you put
the car in park, touch my face.
Cocoa butter still makes me say ok.

Everything gets destroyed
in a single night
and a series of days to come.
A trajectory, an arc, a target hit.

Gun in my face.
Your lover in the doorway
won't let you go.
I see the pinhole of his 9mm;
it mouths I love you.
Behind me I can't see your mouth
say whatever it does to diffuse.
I close the door;
it makes the bullet real.

After, I go
to wipe your cheek.
You flinch.

Your niece holds my wrist
little fingers obsessed with soft arm hair
little fingertips all afternoon play
on the arm of her brother man.
I rest weightless, submerged.
Feels like I'm at the end
of a mostly satisfying life.
I listen to you tell her
not to get too attached
we gotta head back to Leavenworth soon.

Suppose I left.
Suppose I fucked another's man's wife.
Suppose I was getting revenge.
Suppose I'm a weed growing
in the crack of a great prison's bricks.
Suppose I left,
pulling myself from our cement.

One day our niece pulls my arm hair,
one little strand from her brother man,
runs and runs, and runs to her room.
I could see the door closing
in the irises of her eyes,
brown to black, and watery.

As Safe As One Can Get In A Marriage

At the inmate barber shop. Inmate Robinson—pulls a
straight razor. We joke how easy it would be for me to die
sitting in this beat up barber's chair. I remember how before
his life sentence was overturned he'd insert comments
about how hard it must be to marry another guard—a
black woman. *You got it easy, my man. Your wife's got every*
swinging dick wrapped around her fingers. She and you safe.
Robinson's dark forefinger and thumb held my head still.
Don't want to cut ya. The blade scrapes miniscule dead
skin and shaving cream—all in a seamless arc. His hands
as tender as my wife's kisses. I remember how much of an
asshole he was to other guards down in 4 Base 2 Tier Right. I
remember how he first fucked with me: him shuffling along
in his hand and legcuffs, his belly chain snug; me holding his
left arm so he wouldn't fall or fight. After each step forward,
one foot would pause next to his other, forcibly holding me
close. He'd hum the wedding march and ask, *Are we gonna*
fuck tonight? I'd say no, show him the gold on my finger.
Robinson's laugh is slightly different in the barber shop. Less
brick, more gravel. In the mirror I see him smiling with the
straight razor. He's fucking with me again.
Never divorce, man. You'd never survive without her.

Bricks Witness

Bricks witness time served
the leaving and the longing
the you and the me.

Bricks witness the ugly
riot-grin between
I love you / I hate you.

Bricks witness the prison
in all its glory, the prison
of two islands landlocked.

Order in a Season of Storms

Grit teeth / Get your bearing / Plenty of places to hide in prison
Look / Camera zooms on faces / No room to hide in prison

Now I don't know about you / You sure as hell ain't me
It's midnight / The guard cage / Quiet screams in prison

Anal sex / Greasy burnt pine oil / Sweat creeps through bars
Through the protection of darkness / It's really safe in prison

Reading The Exorcist in absolute zero silence / Dim lights
1980's paperback musk / Close enough to bend crosses in prison

Sweat through sheets / Moist fingers making Fibonacci spirals
Squares: book box sink bed cell door block life sentence prison

It's summer here in Kansas / Everybody wants sex / Everybody
Needs that burning / Everybody takes bets on who owns this prison

Guards laugh as eggs fry on basement boiler concrete / Cage free
Brown t-shirts / Pit stains the size of desert salt beds / Hot house

Yeah / You sure as hell ain't free / No way / Inmates be lucky
Rhythm & repetition / They tell me / It's simple-hard here in prison

The French Connection blasts through tube tv speakers / Rank:
Heavys in the front / Bitches in the back / Guards stand in prison

Sergeant Pessant obsesses about who's fucking his wife right now/
Inmate Pessant wonders which guard will wind up next in prison

Caught

So. Here we are, Nuahsor.
Untidy.
Back against prison bars,
salt-stone sweat.

There's a kiss.
Lips.

Our Battle Dress Uniforms, soaked.
Clinging to us in the night.
We're heat in the dark.

Oh! Our hands penetrate space,
fingertips on hips.
Veins throbbing, tensing, stretching our skin.

You sneeze,
asbestos dust lands on our heads.
We laugh, wipe midnight off,

continue to inspect:
handcuffs, legcuffs,
belly chains and black boxes,
cell-block sleeping bodies.
Checkmarks like come-hither fingers.

Off duty's hours away.
We can't wait.
An empty cell.
Inmates snorings set an alarm.

We hold impatience close
to a trickle.
My ear lobe is between your teeth.

The sounds of sleep stop.
Cell's no longer safe.
Starch in our BDUs stick to us,
lets us linger,
allows us to flatten out eros.

Back of the cell block.
Cameras fog on shifts like these.
Can the Guard Commander see us
push against each other in the rear of 7 tier.

Dusty cell block fencing bending,
our boots stomping upon cigarette-break butts.

A piece of your neck hair tongues my mouth,
makes me spit-cough,
makes laugh lines ripple.

An island of prison nights
caught between
husband and wife.

To My Married Self, At Twenty-Four
after Brenda Shaughnessy

If there was more time to love you,
I made it. Without exception, without relief.

Is this what love does? It empties
like a desert river as we walk
hand in hand with subtle thirsts.

If there was more desire to be conjured,
I did it. Without hesitation, without disbelief.

Is that what lovers do? They throw
themselves against each other like
fleshy waves against coastal rock,
the spray of desperation never subsides.

Are my ears not yours to command? They fill
themselves like air in the lungs of newborn finches.

And as I breathe in your breath
I wake to the soft snore of poems.

Is this not the taste of loving?
A bitter pill, slow defeat dissolving,
tastebuds overworked by love's inevitable return.

If I happen to dream of you, of only you,
while you're curled at my side, feet on my belly,
would I want to wake to hold you or
lay still dreaming of the impossible you?

Stomp n Drag

Note: This is used as an offensive formation
to penetrate or to split crowds.
—United States Army Field Manual 3-19.15

At the prison gate we wait
two by two
a procession
soldier to shoulder.
We gaze into each other's eyes.
Our riot gear tight
across our shins
our forearms, elbows, knees.
The flak vest constricting
the rise and fall
of our heartbeats.

(I don't agree
with you
This place
swallows me, swallows you
heart whole down our throats
This place is reaching
like ivy up walls
like shotgun shells
blown apart with trigger fingers.
If you have to leave,
don't run,
don't leave
for war
The desert doesn't
even love you.)

We've trained
incessantly
to love
capsaicin.
On windy days
we're fucked,
too much love
chokes us, leaves
us useless.
Today, there's no crying,
only a wedge
splintering
what's ahead of us.

It's important to note
there's little to say
to sway your mind
to stay your legs, your feet
next to mine. Unison.
In step with the cadence.
You left, you left, your left right left.

Crush & Feel

There's a technique
in loving someone you know
you'll be divorced from some day

Clear—cut

much like a deployment
                a leaving behind
                a kiss every 6 months
                moonlight in the morning
                grasping for you
                the way a mason does
                out of repetition
                faithful to the process

Prison bricks witness a technique too
At Leavenworth there's a way to crush and feel
along the blunt creases of an inmate's uniform
                a way in which fingers bend muscle
                the way knuckles graze the groin
                a way a hand passes over another's heart
                too fast to feel what needs to be felt
                almost as if it wasn't really there

When you left me
on a scorching day in June
you laughed
This heat'll get me ready for Afghanistan…
will you miss me
I winced

I remember the technique of gone
the tongue twisting tiny truths like bits of brick
My teeth chewing them down
enough to turn any oasis into desert

An inmate stands in front of me
honest   naked   feet rooted
on cold concrete
in the inmate bathroom after Sunday visitation

He hands me his brown shirt   brown pants
white socks   white briefs
all smell like perfume
like a wife's kiss
like a wife's breath
like a wife's flesh
Visitation's over and we must
follow procedure
We must crush and feel
though he crushes time like I can't

Gone-ness is
equal measures
snail mail love letters
and slammed landlines

Deployment distance
is a real excuse
for two islands tempted
every night

Today, far away
from any walls I keep
                having dreams of a Fort Leavenworth house
                mowing the front lawn
                edging the edge of the boundary
                of the cement sidewalk
                and the earth
                where your bare foot
                touches my bare foot

7 Base 2 Tier Right

Three eggs sit frying on the cement floor. We laugh so much asbestos dust falls from our nostrils. Now, let me be clear, the eggs don't *fry* fry, but the heat from the boilers underneath the United States Disciplinary Barracks' Special Housing Unit rather quickly congeal clear to white and soft yellow yolk to clammy mustard. Our sergeant snores in the guard cage as prison-duty metal pedestal fans drone a constant waaaaaaaa, like jet engines would, if confined to a small room. We three are neck deep into our eleventh of twelfth 12-hour midnight shift. Yeah, we're scrambled. But the eggs keep solidifying, so much so that they seem fake, like they belong in a window menu. What we should be doing: taking out our hand-sized Folger-Adams keys, inserting them into tier doors, careful not to disturb the sleeping habits of inmates, ants, dust bunnies, and those things so miniscule that they don't have names. We should be looking into each semi-lit cell, watching chests rise and fall. We should be on guard for silence, eyes probing, for hands passing a blade between bars, for toilet water flooding the tier, slit wrists, blood and urine splashed on yolky faces, for the prison waking. But the eggs. Those three fried placid eggs laugh, and demand diligent inspection.

If You Lived Here, You'd Be Home Now

Dear Desert of my Life,

Have you returned from the war?
How was it? What did you do
there in the sand? How come
you never asked?

I am alright. Alone. My own war was short.
How do we endure a word like deployment?

Hey, did you get the toothpaste
and the paddle brush you needed
me to send in a box full of time wasted?
On your Facebook page you look good
with short hair now. So different
than on our wedding day.

Has the nervousness of being away
and back again subsided...
are there still moments you still want me...
here I am. Alone is not a word I want to use
with you...I don't want to use it like dawn...
but every morning I take a shower alone.
I eat alone. I drive to work alone.
I hang out with friends
alone.
(Hey, who is that guy who tagged you
in his Facebook post, his arms around you,
you are smiling...)

The war has left us alone,
are you coming home?

September 12th, 1976

there's ritual in the sound
as if chopping itself
means survival,

the ritual of a blunt blade
cracking apart oak
into uniquely unequal halves,

one half travels back
into the woodpile, breathing
a sigh of relief

the other remains, pleading
with me on the worn stump.
with each axe thump

what words wouldn't I say now
that in winter I'd say to each log
I place into the fire?

a catch 22, a koan.
as if sweat were ashes.
as if flesh and marrow were survival.

an uprooted cluster of one-sided pine
waits for me, waits for my axe.
they wait to warm me in February.

Uncle Sam

You know I used to think
I was the shit.
First in my family
enlisted: Army, active duty
standing in a field stabbing
a rubber dummy in uniform,
bloodshot-rust bayonet
into the heart of a tire.
See how it sucks
in the blade, as easily as a body.
Does blood really make grass grow?
It was barren in that field,
just the white-knuckled movements
of young hands.   Uncle Sam needs you
tattooed under our fingernails.

Your uncle was in the Reserves
my mom said one day after a few
flakes had coated the porch
turning my footprints to slush.
I would be back to basic before they froze,
before I could think I could be wrong:
He never went to war; that doesn't count
These days   it's the seasons
my uncle remembers more than any war.

My uncle killed a man one night.
The man, already half frozen, I imagine
couldn't hear the steel plow
scraping snow from tar.
You see, my uncle was under contract.
Small town safe roads and freedom and the dream.
The man, curled up in a snowstorm,
the fresh blanket of 2am.

Slap-awake
and an arm in the air
and a leg in the snowbank
and the slam of brakes
and a slight skid
and the slow stare backwards,
the mirror red with brake lights.

I never killed a man though
I took an oath to do so.
In 2010, it was all the rage
to be called a combat vet.
Combat   I guess   means madness
I mean   manliness.
It's all the same swerve
into the night   measure oneself
a length of dead-cold work
to be done for
Uncle Sam   Is there such a thing as knowing
you're a real man?

Combat Vet?   *As if killing a man*
gets you better service.

I can't imagine killing a man.
There's a sorrow of unexpectation,
of a weeping every January.
I imagine my uncle imagines
that I'm the lucky one
every time it begins
to snow.

Vaporware

I mean it's like Japan in the 80's up in here—excessive, extravagant restraint. Our naked city spills just the right amount of post techno-climate-feminist theory, like soggy bread crumbs rehydrated for peach-fuzz fanatics. We get hit! In our stereo beat reproductive organs. But Nuahsor and I, we all ready for the isms. The neo-auto-erotic capitalisms, the way-too-out-there- Ponzi-enabled liberalisms, the long-dead-yet-somehow-resurrected-and-always-talked-about-with-a-wave-of-the-hand landmine enthusiasms. Yeah, feels like prison sheets. Automatic and automatically caressing the folds out our streets, the streets with the treats and angel-faced peeps. There's a bar underground us, a barrier between this and that, the staunch stench of human living and the E-womb. Cell block life. I mean each apartment are bars, round-thick and wide, enough to stick it in peep-show eyes. Nuahsor and I live here. She and me cohabitate. We don't make babies; it's passé. A hardcore sin. Who'd want to survive in this shit anyway. There's a hurricane coming, a whopper they say. Damn! Me and her just made it through the last-ditch-effort-swallowed-sinkhole brink. Last week, fires. Last month, two cities abandoned, underwater. We hear beech trees screaming. Everywhere I close my eyes, blurring. I can hear the future gurgling. It sounds like dial-up, unnatural and anticipatory. Like gills, man. Heavy breathing, bitter-skipping across broken concrete lakes. Nuahsor believes we're gonna die tomorrow. I kinda agree, kinda relieved.

Guard Duty at Dusk

I almost died in prison
20 years ago. Well, almost
is a tricky word. It sits
on the fence like a cat
in a box, like a catch-22 handshake.
It's almost a risk
to let that word hang.

And yet, most of the time almost is dead.
In the memory of me,
a prison guard reminiscing
the razor's edge.
I get paper-cut shivers—
brain-squeezing, bisecting
all my tiny barely-living moments.

It's best not to think
about the spit fists,
about the eyes playing
the accordion of my life
before them. Squeezing
as sharp as a blink.

In between almost
hides like a corner,
like dusk.

Do you remember me
saying I almost died?

Growth
after Tanikawa Shuntaro

age forty
I know not a thing about the future

age forty-three
I only know the present as thinning hair

age forty-seven
I see my ex-wife; she has a family

age forty-seven
I see ink drying on the very last limb

age forty-seven
I see a chickadee's a dee dee dee

age forty-eight
Its song smudges the long winter I now know well

age forty-nine
Those around me start to die, in groups of me

age fifty
I unexpectedly see Death

age fifty
I give him a high five

combat:peace

*a meditation on the
passing of Thich Nhat Hanh*

five novices kneel
five recruits sit

ten heads are shaved
basic   for training

reciting ten precepts
oathing seven values

transform all suffering
     obey all orders

are you part of us
ordained and loved

are you one of us
brave and bold

the symbolic removal
of hair   of fear   of self

and I can't stop continuing.
all I see is an apron of tears

in the future   will we
have the need for

soldiers   or
buddhists   or

for rituals in which hair
pillows to the floor

Synthetic Cow's Milk

A robot couple zeros down
        a broke road, tar and gravel and grass indistinguishable.
            They don't care, the one lane road
                  was abandoned before they breathed
                      19% Oxygen.

Their skinless digits feel for each other's
        coldness in the late autumnal afternoon
            G2V-type starlight.
                    Radiation holds at 1,370 W/m^2

Metallic hands clasp, a ting spooks the cows. Their rustless
mouths moo.   Afraid-milk tastes oily.

The couple remembers:

                the teats slope down like stalactites,
                hard-deliberate, soft robotic hands
                fitting under the udder, gleaming
                shimmer-code with each tug-stroke
                metal-milk hits the bucket, ting.

The soot in the air's at .4%; in the cities the carbon-flesh burn
themselves.   Drip, drip, drip to dust.

The cows and couple meet at stone-fence, greet each other.
              A squishy scraping sound
              cuds in unison, content. CH4
              levels low enough, measured
              in machine breath, milked
              like last days on Earth.

The Impermanence of Being Alone

forget-me-not

I invite my young cousin and his girlfriend
to walk the coastline beyond Winslow Park.
We climb down the tree-root-step embankment,
let our toes recede within the soft sand of the tide's
outgoing wake. Living crabs remain still like the
dead ones, until prodded by the removal of a perfect
stone to skip on the bare skin of the Atlantic.

I ask him *Which do you prefer to live*
next to? The forest or the ocean?
He laughs, slants his back slightly, winds his arm up.
The forest, but this isn't too bad either.

And I think how I could have had a son
like him, a daughter like her.
I watch them play at their future
and know that my own receding tide
is like a September stone skipped.

marigold

My niece and I share a joint at the summit
of Bradbury Mountain. The daytime moon
greets us with a wink and we laugh.
October is a good time for family.

Our legs hang over a large glacial remnant,
our feet approve of the opposing gravity
and she asks *What's it like being forty?*
I tell her *It's like getting out of prison.*

I often think that my own daughter
would have been like her—wily, unafraid,
easy to talk with. I recount to her my dreams
of a daytime moon and a wisp
of laughing smoke and a mountain.
I warn myself that right now
seems like a leaf turning red as it falls.

chrysanthemum

I forgot today is family day
at the art museum at Bowdoin College.
An attendant asks me if the boy
playing hide and seek
under the Renoir is mine.
The boy stops to hear my answer.
He's not mine, I've no children.
Oh, I'm sorry—says the attendant.
Me too.

The father in me fidgets.
Eons from now the sun will swallow
a family name easily forgotten.

Sometimes I think I am a man
realizing I am two different days
sharing the same calendar square.
Some days I feel I am November,
and that my only children will be me.

Jonathan Pessant is a Maine poet. He graduated from the Stonecoast MFA program at the University of Southern Maine, where he was the poetry editor for the *Stonecoast Review*. Jonathan is an Army veteran and served as a Corrections NCO at Fort Leavenworth, Kansas from 1998-2005. His poems have appeared in *Collateral Journal, Pedestal Magazine, Stonecoast Review*, and most recently in Milltown Press' GI Days: *An Anthology of Military Life* and at Military Experience & Arts' As You Were: *The Military Review*.

9 798888 387962

A Thought

Kendra Temple

Contents

1-prologue

Have you ever thought about death?

Not just about death but something else.

You see. Why do we humans think there's just life and death?

Maybe there's something third?

Maybe there's something in between?

Why do we humans think there's a thing and there's a thing that's opposite that thing.

What if there are two opposites?

What if there are three?

Or more?

You see, I don't get that.

It seems logic but when you think about it you realise.

Who said there are just two sides?

This goes on and on in my head and I can't wrap my mind around it.

Why are we here? Why are we alive? What does even mean we are alive? There could be so many other things. I think there has to be a reason. There has to be a point.

Okay. We are alive. And then we die. What's the point? Becouse I don't see it.

I'm trying to tell you that there has to be a reason why we are here.

Eight million people just appeared on Earth. I think here's something going on. Because what's the reason we are here? There has to be one.

I feel like we are in a game and life is just an illusion.

Maybe we get answers when we die. If death even exists.

I guess we'll see.

2

Sometimes I think it would be easier if I died young since when I'm young I haven't experienced many things that I would miss if I died. Because when I'll be old and I'll have to die, there would be some things that I would like to experience again, but wouldn't get the chance to.

Is this what everyone thinks?

I haven't been on a plane before. But now I am.

A few hours later I'm walking out of an airport where my dad should be waiting for me. I don't remember the last time I saw him. He was supposed to be dead.

And now I'll have to live with my dad and his family. I just found out I have a twin brother too.

I finally spot my dad who's holding a sign with my name. That's so weird. I'm surprised he even remembers it.

"Valeri?"

"Dad?"

He leans for a hug but I step away. His smile slowly fades.

"Please don't touch me," I mutter.

Who does he think he is? First he leaves and makes my mom believe he died. Because of that she started using drugs until she overdosed and died. Then the police tells me my father's alive and he has a family. And now I'm here before him and he just expects me to be okay with it? To forget all the shit?

We just awkwardly stand there for a few seconds until he clears his throat "I think we should go."

"Yeah, we should." I say and open walk past him.

"How was the flight?" He asks after a few minutes of driving in a complete silence.

"It was okay," I shortly say.

We drive for at least an hour until I catch a sight of the sea. There's sun getting set right behind it.

It looks gorgeous.

I wish I could paint it right now right here.

After a few minutes first houses appear. Not houses. Mansions.

I can't believe some people have all this money and some people need to work two jobs so we can keep ourselves alive. It's not fair.

We finally pull in the courtyard of a really big house. I have never seen such a big house as this. My jaw drops. My dad lived here all this time and I was there almost dying every single day. I can't believe this. I can't believe him.

Dad parks the car and opens the door. I follow him into the house.

A few days ago I was dying because I didn't have money. And now I'm suddenly rich.

I sigh and enter.

There's a huge closet filled with a lot of shoes and coats. My dad says I should take off my shoes. I do. He also says I should leave my luggage here. Too bad I don't have one.

So I follow him in the kitchen.

I freeze when I see food. When I say food, I mean a huge amount of food.

"Take a sit," my dad says.

I slowly move closer to the table and sit down.

"Alex should be home soon." I know he wants to start a conversation.

"Okay," I say like I don't care. I actually really don't care. I don't care about this stupid house. I don't care about my dad. I don't care about my so called brother. I don't care about anything. Because I feel nothing. When I look at this food I can't move my hand to get any. The struggle is too big. Memories run through my head. Memories of my mom. How hard she tried to make my life perfect but with years lost herself in heroin. And I even knew back then it won't end well. But I couldn't help her. I didn't know how to. And then she died. I used to tell myself I will never be like her. I will never be broken and I will try to make my life good. And I am trying. But I can't. I feel like I failed. I failed. And I told myself I wasn't going to.

I pick up some food and bring it to my mouth. I chew it slowly and struggle to swallow.

It broke me. Her death. It broke me so much I can't get myself to eat. I feel like I don't deserve it. I convinced myself I will not let my mom down but I did. I was out drinking that night and when I came home she was there.

On the couch. Frozen. I thought she was sleeping and I tried to shake her awake but she didn't move. She wasn't breathing. I called an ambulance and they took her away. She passed that night.

I come back to reality when I hear front door open. A moment later a guy comes into the kitchen. He's tall and his hair a little lighter thank mine.

I stand up.

His eyes widen in excitement when he notices me. "Umm hey, I'm Alex. You must be Valeri, right? It's so good to finally meet you. Dad talked about you a lot." He says and wraps his hands around me. I don't know what to do so I hug him back. After a few moments he pulls away and smiles down at me.

"Alex, I told you to not bother her too much. She must be really tired. Why don't you show Valeri her room? We can continue tomorrow."

"Alright," he says. He looks annoyed. "Follow me." he gently takes my hand and leads out of the kitchen. We walk down the hall, up the stairs into another hallway. There's two doors here.

"Okay so here is my room if you need anything. And here..." he opens another door. "...is your room."

I enter the room right behind Alex.

I look at the space. It's quite a big room. Bigger than at home. It has huge windows and a bed. The walls are white and there's no decorations. But I like it.

"Do you like it? I didn't know what you like and what are your interests so I left everything white. But you can always come to me, if you want to change your room, paint the walls or whatever." He looks at me.

I don't know what to say. I honestly don't care what my room looks like. "I like it." I say. I hate that my voice sounds so monotone. I just don't know how to show emotions. Sometimes I want to die when that happens. When I'm really happy about something and I don't know how to show it. It's so annoying.

"I'm so happy to hear that. Come here." He waves at me. I go after him and enter the bathroom. This shit is huge. There's a bath and a shower and everything.

"If you need anything just tell me, okay?"

"Okay." I agree and we go back in the bedroom.

Alex opens the door and turns to look at me. "I'm really sorry about what happened. I don't know how to help but if you ever need somebody to talk to I'm here. I know it's hard and everything but don't keep things to yourself. It will kill you." He sadly smiles at me.

Wow. Someone actually cares.

"Thank you." I say.

"There's a party tomorrow if you want to come with me. It's at my friend's house and there will be others too. It'll be fun. But I understand if you want to rest."

"I- umm... I'll think about it."

What was I supposed to say? Yes? The last time I was at a party it didn't end well.

"Okay" He says. "You'll meet my friends if you come. They're so excited to see you."

"I'm glad." I say. I fucking hate how I sound. I fucking hate it!

"Good night."

"Night."

Alex closes the door and I sigh and fall back onto the bed. I can't help but let the tears come free. How could I be so stupid?! I'm so fucking stupid! I hate it! I hate myself so fucking much! How could I let this happen? I was such a shitty daughter. I cover my mouth with my hand so I don't make much noise. I'm so fucking stupid. I should've been there. I let her down. I fucking let her down. I failed. I cover myself with a sheet and sob into the pillow. I can't do it. I can't do it anymore. She's dead. And I'm still here. I shouldn't be. It hurts so much. It hurts so damn much. I don't deserve anything.

I pull myself up so I'm sitting on the bed and take my bag. I open the front pocket.

My vision is blurry because of my tears but I would always know how they look like.

Here they are.

Pills.

I put a few of them in my hand. I bring my hand to my mouth. I put them on my tongue. I swallow them. I lay down. I close my eyes.

And let them consume me.

AN: -word count- 1516 I'm kind of proud on myself.Please let me know how you feel about this chapter.The next ones will be more interesting but check TWs.

3

I wake up in sweat. I look around. It's still dark outside.

Shit. I can't breathe. Not again.

Not again.

I thought the pills were going to make it better but I guess they didn't. Taking them from my bag I stumble to the bathroom and fall down the floor with my back to the door. I let the tears fall.

I can't breathe. I can't breathe. I can't breathe.

My hands are shaking. And my whole body.

And I can't hear anything. There's just ringing in my ears. And everything is blurry.

Taking two pills I lift them and with shaking hand put them in my mouth. I swallow them whole and lay down on the floor.

Please help.

I stay there for around ten minutes 'till the pills take in. I just lay there for a couple of minutes more until I stand up. The room is spinning. Everything is spinning.

I stumble to the sink and put my hands on it. Lifting my face up as I look at myself in the mirror. My black hair falls down my back and my hazel eyes are staring back at me.

I splash some cold water on my face and look at myself again.

Everybody always said I'm pretty. I know I don't look bad.

I head back to the bedroom and lay down.

The walls and a wardrobe and windows are spinning.

And I spin with them.

~~~

I spent the whole day in the bedroom and tonight is the night of the party that Alex was talking about. I don't know what to expect. Probably a lot of alcohol.

It reminds me of that night. I was at some party. Everyone was drunk including me. I was standing in the kitchen. Music was loud I barely heard anything. Some guy was talking to me. I don't remember his name or what he was saying. I was wasted.

Soon it was time to go. I don't drive a car. Never had the money. So I walked. On the way I drank lots of water since I knew I'll have to take care of mom when I get home.

It was cold even though it was Summer. I just finished junior year. That's why I was at that party. Never had a lot of friends in high school so I went there just to get drunk or eat something.

When I opened the front door of my house I quietly walked in. I knew I'll see my mom passed out on the couch with a drink in her hand. I entered the living room and the first thing I saw was a bag of white powder.

Not again.

I turned to my mom finding her asleep as I thought I would.

I approached her and touched her hand. It was cold. And when I say cold I mean really cold. I quickly checked if she was breathing. She wasn't. Then I checked if her heart was beating. It wasn't either.

Freezing cold went through my body. I couldn't believe it. I couldn't believe that was really happening. I was out drinking and she was at home dying.

When I got my senses back I took my phone and called an ambulance.

I could barely speak. I could barely even think.

They said it was too late...

"Valeri?"

I realise I zoned out.

"Valeri?" Someone's knocking on my door.

"Yeah?" I call out.

"Are you ready? Can I come in?" A raspy voice asks. Alex came into my room a few hours ago asking if I decided about the party.

"Okay."

Alex opens the door and looks at me.

"You look stunning." He looks good too but I don't know how to tell him. Yeah, people would say it was easy giving compliments but it wasn't for me so I just stood there staring at myself in the mirror.

He's wearing just some sweats and a hoodie.

"Thanks." I smile at him.

I turn back to the mirror.

I feel dead. On the inside.

I think I look good though. My black dress matches my hair and brings out the color of my eyes. My nose piercing is glittering in the lights of the room.

"We should go." He says.

"Sure." I take my phone and follow him downstairs.

"Dad is working late." He says and leads me out to the car. It looks like he has his own.

It's black and it looks really expensive.

We get in and he drives out of the driveway. "It's just a quick ride."

"Okay." I say.

"You drive?" He asks quickly looking at me before he focuses back on the road.

"No." I simply say.

"Why not? You're 17." He gives me a curious glance.

"Yeah."

"I've never had time or money, you know? There's been a lot of shit going on." I say not wanting to say more.

"You wanna talk about it?" He looks worried.

"No, it's okay."

I turn to the window. It's already dark outside. Memories flood my mind again and I don't even realise tears are threatening to fall out of my eyes.

Alex seems to notice and takes my hand in his. "You want to go back?"

I think about it. "No, I think the party will help me keep my mind off things for a bit, you know?" I whisper not trusting my voice.

He just squeezes my hand a little tighter. "I'd tell you to stay with me the whole time but I don't think I can do that. You must keep your phone with you, though, just in case."

"Well I think I'll stay with you becouse I don't know anyone, if that's okay."

"Of course."

We soon pull into a driveway of some big house. As soon as I step out of the car a loud music fills my ears.

Alex leads me to the house. It looks like some people are already drunk. Can't wait to be like them.

We step inside. The music is even louder here. I can barely hear Alex when he says in my ear.

"If you want to leave just tell me, okay? I'll get you home."

I nod and follow him. He's making his way through the crowd with me on his heels.

We come into a little less crowded room. It looks like Alex knows where he's going becouse we soon approach a couple of guys sitting on the floor laughing about something.

When they see him they both stand up and give him some 'bro' hugs or whatever.

Even though I keep myself in his shadow he suddenly turns to me and brings me forward.

"Sooo I want you to meet someone."

They all look at me. That's kinda creepy.

"This is my sister Valeri."

"Oh my god, this is her? Why the fuck didn't you mention she's so fucking pretty?" The blond one sighs.

I smile up at him. "Thanks." I mutter.

"Wait, you're real?"

"No"

"Waittttt are you a ghost?" He turns to the others. "I told you ghosts exist."

"She's not a ghost, Lach. She's real. Alive." Alex reassures him.

"Yeahh but she said-" Lach continues.

"It was a joke."

He just blankly stares at me for a few seconds.

"Oh. I guess that makes sense." He looks sad.

"Don't mind Lach. He's kinda wasted." The other one says rolling his eyes.

I chuckle.

The blond one is still looking at me with his mouth wide open. My brother brings his hand up and shuts it.

"Guysss I think I just met my new best friend." Lach says with his finger pointed at me.

My brother and his friend giggle at that and I join in.

The one with brown hair introduces himself to me. He tells me his name's Kian.

"You two look so much alike." He adds looking from me to Alex and back.

"Wait, where the fuck is Zach? He was supposed to be here a while ago." My brother asks.

"Ohhh he went to get some drinks for us right before you came. You know, our hidden bottles of vodka." Kian whispers the last part winking at me.

Interesting.

We all sit down on the couch.

Lach sits next to me with a wide smile on his face.

The guy they were just talking about enters the room with some bottles in his hands.

"Zachhhyyyyy!" Lach jumps off the couch and points at me. "This is Alex's sister. You see her?"

"Yeah, Lach I think you should lie down for a bit though." Zach says with his gorgeous green eyes still fixed on me.

Wait I've seen him before. Or maybe I'm just making that up. And his eyes-

Lach literally lies on the floor with a big ass smile still on his face.

What the fuck-

The other guy steps over him and approaches me.

"Zachary."

Zachary

Before I could say anything, another guy enters the room.

Do they even have any girl friends?

"Heyyyyy." An obviously drunk guy says. He sits down on the couch opposite me.

But I can't unnotice how his eyes travel over my body quite a few times within conversation with his friends and I suddenly feel very exposed.

AN: -word count- 1538I hope you liked this chapter. I honestly don't know how to feel about this book but I'll try to make it good.

4

We've been laughing and drinking for hours now and I'm feeling a bit dizzy becouse of the alcohol but I can still feel that drunk guy's gaze on my dress. It makes me uncomfortable and I keep fidgeting with my rings.

I try to stay calm but after a few more minutes I can't do it anymore.

"Hey, Zach, where's the bathroom?" I ask him since I found out we're at his house.

"Up the stairs second door on the left. I can go with you if you don't want to go alone." Zach smiles at me.

"No, that's okay." I stand up and hurry up the stairs. I still feel someone's eyes on my back.

There's not much people up here. Just some couples making out.

I make my way to the bathroom and lock myself in it.

I lean on the closed door behind me and take a deep breath. Opening my eyes I look at myself in the mirror infront of me.

My lips are cracked from biting them. I didn't even realise I was doing that.

I just stare at myself for a while. Am I overreacting? He was looking, right? But he's not the first guy to ever do that. I shouldn't be feeling so anxious.

Without thinking I put my hand in my pocket.

Wait-

I'm wearing a dress.

And it does not have pockets.

And I do not have my pills.

I must've left them on my nightstand.

Fuck.

I search the drawers under the sink and every shelf in this bathroom. And nothing's here. Who doesn't have at least one package of pills in their bathroom?

Shit.

I take some deep breaths and try to sort myself out.

The urge though-

I unlock the bathroom door and step on the hallway.

While I'm turning to the stairs a someone brushes my hip with their hand.

I quicken my pace and head downstairs.

Before I reach the last step I turn my head around.

Fuck.

I'm sobered up in a moment.

I walk to the couches where the boys are still joking around.

"You good?" Alex asks me. Now everyone's staring at me.

"Yeah, why?"

"You look pale." He says worried.

"I'm just tired. I didn't sleep well last night." A half-truth.

"Let's go home then." He stands up and takes my hand. "I'll see you tomorrow, yeah?" He says to his friends and gives them some 'bro' hugs again.

They all say goodbyes to me and Lach of course has to give me a hug. I love this guy.

Before we exit the room I turn back and look at Zachary. I catch him already looking at me with his green eyes again. Is that him?

No Valeri there's hundreds of Zachary's. It'd be a too big coincidence.

But he looks so familiar.

Once we make it to the car I'm already sober.

My brother turns up some music and we pull out of the driveway.

I zone out again. What if he does it again? What if he does something more?

Alex turns music down and gives a quick look my way before focusing back on the road.

"I'll make you something for dinner, okay? You barely ate anything today."

Is it that obvious?

"I'm not hungry." I mumble.

"Okay, but you'll eat something whether you like it or not." He states.

We spend the rest of the ride in silence and soon pull infront of our house.

Alex unlocks the door and I go up to my room without saying a word.

I walk too my closet and take some grey sweats and a black hoodie.

As I'm walking toward the bathroom I notice the pills I forgot on my nightstand.

I grab them and head into the bathroom where I put them in the drawer under my period products.

I undress and drop the, now feeling dirty dress on the floor.

I step into the shower and turn on the water.

Just a little warmer.

Now water is burning my skin and with that it takes all my thoughts and pain away. I let it drop down my body and I don't even realise hot tears are streaming down my face until a loud sob escapes my mouth.

I cover it with my hands and quietly sob into them as I break down. The hot water burns my skin making the pain in my head go away.

I don't know how much time I spend in the shower and when I calm myself down I turn off the water.

As soon as I open the shower door and step on the cold tiles, steam comes up from my skin into the cool air.

I know I shouldn't be having hot showers like that but they just make me feel better.

I splash my face with cold water making all traces of crying dissapear. I dry my hair and start dressing up.

There are healed scars all over my wrists that you can't notice if you're not looking for them. A constant reminder of my past. All the pain.

It all started when I started enjoying the cat scratches. It made me feel so good. That went on and on for months until I realised I could do it with a sharper. That felt even better. I did it every day telling myself just one more time.

I've never reached out for help. I have never told anyone.

Except for one person.

Him.

He always listened to me. He always gave me a hug when I needed one. He always cheered me up. He always made me feel better.

And now he's gone. I don't know where he is or with who.

He just disappeared one day and never came back.

And I was all alone again. And there wasn't anyone anymore who could stop me. So I continued doing it.

Don't get me wrong, I've been clean for two months now.

It got better two years ago. Just a few scratches every few weeks. But I started doing something worse.

I took the pills for the first time when I was 15. They helped me keep things off my mind and I could live without a worry for a few hours.

And now I can't stop.

He would be disappointed in me if he saw me now.

I take one last look in the mirror and head back in the bedroom.

I quietly open the door. Alex is downstairs cooking.

I run down the stairs and make my way to the table.

He's turned with his back to me.

"Hey." I mutter.

"Oh, hey, Valeri. I thought you were sleeping since you didn't come down to eat. I actually waited for you if you appeared by any chance. You want some?"

"Sure." I sit down.

He brings food to the table. Pasta carbonara. My stomach growls.

He laughs. "I knew you were hungry."

I laugh and roll my eyes.

We start eating and I remember that I haven't seen dad since yesterday when he picked me up at the airport.

"Where's dad? I didn't see him today." I say.

"Oh. He has just texted me saying he's with his family." He shrugs with his shoulders.

"What? What do you mean?"

"He hasn't told you?" Shock is written over his face. "He has a wife and children. He asked me if I wanted to go with him a few years ago but I declined. And he spends most of his time there, so he won't be home for at least a few weeks."

"So you live alone most of the time?"

"No, Zach is always here. He doesn't have much family either so he stays here a lot. He's my best friend and in some kind of way a brother if you know what I mean."

I do know.

"Why is he not here now?"

"Oh, He's staying with Kian for a few days since you're here."

"I'm so sorr-" I start apologising.

"No, No, I didn't mean it like that. He didn't want to make you feel uncomfortable." He smiles.

Wow.

"Well, don't let me stop you from Zachary being here. I don't mind him." I say. He really didn't have to do that. I was the one who came here.

"Alright, if you're sure."

"I am."

We joke around while we eat. But suddenly he looks like something is bothering him.

"What's wrong?" I ask.

He's quiet for a bit until he continues. "What was she like?"

"Who?"

"Our mother." He speaks quietly and I realise I didn't think about her for the whole dinner.

But what am I supposed to tell him?

I clear my throat. "She was...umm- she was a good mom for a few years but I don't remember those since I was little. But umm..dad probably told you about her, or?

"No, he actually didn't say anything." He says confused.

"What? He didn't?" I stare into my plate.

I take a deep breath. "Then she started drinking and she didn't give me any attention anymore. And it got worse..." My voice breaks a little.

Alex comes around the table and hugs me. I squeeze myself into his arms but I don't cry. I don't think there's any tears left.

AN: -word count- 1548Should I do longer or shorter chapters?

I hope it was interesting!Please comment what you think :)

Thank youuu and I'll hopefully post the next chapter in a few days since I have a lot schoolwork to do.

Have a nice day<33 byee

5

It's been two days since our conversation with Alex about our mom and Zach.

I stayed most of the time in my room not doing anything. I stole some books from Alex and I'm reading one now. It's getting dark outside.

I'm deep in the story when a knock startles me back into present.

"Can I come in?" I hear my brother's voice.

I quickly shove the book under the pillow. Getting up from the bed I stop for a few seconds because black dots take my vision away. Coming back to reality I open my bedroom door.

"Hey." I smile at Alex.

Please don't know about me stealing your books.

"Hey." He says back. "Zach is coming today and he's staying for a while. I just wanted to make sure if it's okay again."

I let out a breath.

"Yeah, that's okay. Where will he be staying?"

"I just told you." I'm the one who winks at him this time.

He smirks at me.

I think I'm nervous.

"Wait I completely forgot about pizza. It's probably already cold. Damn it." He stands up and pulls me with him."Come on. Let's go downstairs."

I shove all the books under my bed again and go after Zachary.

When I come into the kitchen the smell of pizza consumes me but Zach isn't here.

I find him on the couch in the living room with a slice of pizza in his hand.

He taps the place besides him and I sit down.

"Take as much as you want."

I look at it and immediately get the urge to throw up.

"I'd rather not. I'm not hungry right now." I mutter and pull a blanket over me.

"Alex said you didn't eat anything today."

"I wasn't hungry."

"I hardly believe that."

I finally get myself to take a slice just because I want him to let go of it.

I take a bite and swallow it.

"What do you want to watch?" Zach asks with a remote in his hand.

"Whatever you want."

"Oh my god. You're just like Alex. He never knows what to pick."

I laugh at him.

"Then you pick." I say.

We end up watching some random movie but get bored in the middle of it.

I can feel his eyes on me throughout the whole movie.

I think there's some tension between us. But I don't know what it is so I just ignore him.

The pizza I ate is running through my head and I feel like throwing up again.

Did I eat to much?

I don't even realise I started fidgeting with my ring until Zach puts his palm over mine calming me down.

The movie has just ended and we just sit there in silence with our hands locked.

We hear the front door open. I put my hand out of Zachary's as Alex comes to the living room where we are.

"Guess what?" My brother says as soon as he enters the room.

"What?" Zach says with a sigh and rolls his eyes.

"We are going on vacation. We'll stay at Madelin's for a week."

Zach stands up. "Wait, for real? Just like last year?"

"Yeah." Alex now turns to me. "And you will come with us."

"Who's Madelin?" I ask half asleep. They seem to notice and smile at me.

"A friend of ours. She's super nice and can't wait to meet you."

"When is it?" Zach asks.

"We're going there on Friday and you know how Madelin is so there will be a lot of parties. And guess who'll come with the rest of us." He pauses. "Her fucking cousin and his shitty friendgroup."

"Wait what the fuck? You for real? Why?"

"I don't know, man, I just know Madelin's not happy about it either."

"Who would be." Zach snorts.

And I drift off.

~~~

I wake up. The sun is shining through the window and I decide today will be a good day. I put on some sweats and head downstairs.

I hear voices coming from the kitchen and it makes my day even better.

"Good morning." I say as I enter the kitchen.

"Morning." They both say.

I sit down at the table and as soon as I see food my smile fades.

"You okay?" Alex asks.

"Yepp, I'll just go change. Be right back." I hurry back upstairs.

Fuck fuck fuck.

They made me breakfast. I mean it's nice but I just can't. And they saw I'm in a good mood so I can't say I feel sick.

Fuck why is this happening?

I change my clothes and brush my teeth taking as much time as I can. But I know I'll have to face them. Face it.

I can do this.

And I will.

I put a smile on my face and head back down.

"...tell her. She's not okay. She barely eats."

"But she's better now. Did you see her smile? I'm not saying she's okay, Alex. And I can help her either way."

"Alright. Do what you think is the best. But you can't keep it like that forever."

"Yeah, I know." Zach sighs.

When I know their conversation is over I go down the stairs making as much noise as I can.

As I enter the kitchen Alex clears his throat and Zach is staring out of the window.

I can do it.

"I'm going to Lachlan's. I'll see you there." Zachary says and quickly leaves the kitchen.

Alex sits down next to me.

I can do it.

"You okay?" My brother asks looking at me.

I just nod.

"You know you're beautiful." He strokes my hair.

I nod again.

"Valeri talk to me." He whispers. "Please."

"It's just..." I swallow. "...mom. I feel like it's my fault."

"It's not your fault." He says softly.

"If I wasn't drunk-"

"It's not your fault." He hugs me and I lean my head against his chest.

~~~

An hour later we are in front of Lach's house. As soon as we enter someone jumps on me almost knocking me off.

"Heyy." Lach says holding me to him.

"Hey? Are you drunk?"

"Nope. I'm just so happy to see you." He smiles down at me.

I smile back.

He leads me to what looks like a living room and there's around 5 people.

Alex, Zach, Kian, Lach who's next to me and two girls.

We sit down and I look from Alex to Zach.

They exchange a look.

What were they talking about?

"This is my best friend Valeri. Also Alex's sister. Twin sister, actually."

"Oh my god. She's even prettier than you described her, Lach." The one with brown long wavy hair and brown eyes says.

"Thanks."

She and her friend walk over to me.

"I'm Ayna and this is Mers."

They both hug me.

And I feel loved.

AN: -word count- 1561I hope it's not to obvious what Alex and Zach were talking about.Soo what do you think?Next few chapters will be interesting.

Also check TWs if you haven't already. They're written in the story description.

Can someone explain what this voting thing is because I have no idea??▢

I love youuu all byee!!

"Yeahh and I'm so excited." I smile at the thought. "They'll be here in a few minutes."

"Well, have fun." He puts the dishes into a dishwasher. "Be careful and have your phone with you, okay?" He says as he pulls me into his arms. I put my hands around his waist and breath in his smell.

So familiar...

We stay like that until we hear a car pull into the driveway. I step away and take my bag.

"When will you be home?" Zachary calls out.

"I'll text you." I yell as I slam the front door.

I run down the stairs to the car.

"Heyy how are you?" Ayna asks from the passenger seat.

I put my elbows on either of their seats.

"I feel so good. You?" I look from Ayna to Mers.

"We're so excited for the vacations. It will be the same as it was last year and we had so much fun." Mers says. "And now you'll be there as well and that makes it even better." She smiles at me.

I lean back in my seat and sigh. We drive for a few minutes before I remember what I wanted to ask them.

"I have a question."

"Yeah?" They both say.

"It's about Zach."

Silence.

"Wait are you into him? He has never showed interest in anyone. But the way he looks at you-"

"Oh god no. That's not what I wanted to ask you."

"Then what is it?" They exchange looks.

"Did he always live here? Or has he moved?"

I don't miss the way they freeze at my question.

"Yes, he was always here." But they don't look in my eyes when they say that.

I brush it off though. It would be too big of a coincidence and if they say he was born here then I believe. There's no reason they would be lying.

"Oh." I'm kind of disappointed. I don't know what I expected. I think I was hoping for too much and now...

I look out the window.

I just miss him so much. I've thought of him every single day. And every time I relapsed. I was always thinking how disappointed he would be in me right now.

But then I stopped hoping. And now I came here and this hope came back onto the surface and now I feel like something in me broke again.

"Why didn't you ask him, though?" Ayna curiously stares at me.

"I don't know."

"Wait you know someone named Zachary or Zach or whatever?" Mers asks wondering.

"Ye. My best friend. I mean we aren't anymore but... yeah." I smile at the thought.

"So you thought it was our Zach?"

"I mean not that I thought. I just hoped I guess. He reminds me of him so much. The way he looks and how he acts. Everything." I shrug with my shoulders and my cheeks redden. This is embarrassing.

"Oh wow."

"Yeah, it doesn't matter." I say quietly. "Forget about it."

"No. He sounds nice." They smile at me but something is off.

We park our car infront of a huge shopping center.

I excitedly get out of the car. This shit is big.

I fall into step with Ayna and Mers.

Ayna interlocks our hands and we enter the mall. There's so many people and it makes me anxious but I try to forget it.

"Where are we going first?"

"We should buy bikinis for this weekend. Oh my god I can't wait." Mers squeals.

That makes me even more nervous. I just wanted to normally hang out.

But Ayna saves me when she says "We should wait for Madelin."

"Oops I completely forgot." Mers. "We can go eat while we are waiting. Let's text her and she can meets us there."

No.

"Yess I'm literally starving." Ayna tells us.

"I'm not really hungry but we can go if you want to." I say and smile at them.

"Sure, we can get something on the way back home if you'll be hungry then."

"Okay."

We walk into McDonald's and go order.

Ayna and Mers have already picked what they'll eat and now they turn to me.

"Do you want anything?"

"No, thanks. I'm good."

"Alright. Then this is everything." Ayna turns back to the ordering machine.

We find a table in the corner and sit down.

"So, Valeri, what do you think about Lach?" Mers asks with a wink.

"Uhh-...I don't know. He's really... energetic, I guess."

"Yeah he is always like that." Mers laughs out. "But you should see him wasted."

"I already have."

"Wait for real?" Ayna wonders.

"Yup and he thought I was a ghost." I can't help but chuckle as I say that.

There's a moment of silence.

"Ain't no way." Ayna says as she bursts out laughing.

I can't help but smile myself.

After a couple of minutes they get their food.

"You sure you don't want anything?" Mers glances at me.

"No, no it's okay."

"Alright but if you want just take some."

While they're eating they tell me about last year's vacations and it sounds so much fun. I'm really excited but anxious as well. I don't know what I'll do about swimming.

The scars on my arms have almost faded but the ones of my thighs...I knew people would see them on my wrists so I've done it on my legs.

But now...

"Valeri."

"Yeah?" I stutter as I come back into present.

"You okay?" There look worried.

"Yeah." I give them a reassuring smile.

They don't look sure.

"Heyyy."

A girl with dyed red hair is standing over our table.

"Holy shit, M." Mers and Ayna stand up and jump into that girl's arms.

"I missed you so much."

"Where the hell have you been?" Mers asks as they pull away.

"With my piece of a shit cousin." Her eyes land on me and she smiles.

"Heyy. You're Valeri, right?" She asks as they all sit down.

"Yup."

"I'm Madelin. I've been waiting to meet you." Her eyes travel over my face and outfit. "You look so much like Alex."

"I've heard that before." I smile.

"Wait you were at your cousin?"

"Yes sadly." She rolls her eyes. "He came with me. And his friends aka jerks too."

"What the actual fuck? They're here?"

"Yes somewhere around."

They all make faces.

Ayna and Mers finish eating and we head out of McDonald's.

We are joking around while we walk through the shopping center. We go in some other shops.

We follow Mers until we come to the right one.

They're searching through bikinis and I just stand there.

"Ey, Valeri, I think these would look so good on you." Madelin says with black ones in her hands. "You should try them on."

"Yeah, they're nice."

As they pick some too we go try them on.

I let out a breath when we go into separate cabins even though we have to try them on over our underwear.

I undress and look at myself in the mirror. I quickly try the bikinis on and they fit me.

Madelin was right. They fit me so much and I really like them.

I put them off and dress again into my clothes because I don't want them to rush into my cabin to see if they look okay.

I wait for them outside the cabins.

The first to come out is Madelin.

"Soooo will you take them?" She sounds so excited.

"Yes. You?"

"Oh my god yes I can't wait to wear them."

I let out a laugh.

After a few minutes Mers and Ayna come out of one of the cabins.

One.

"What the fuck. You were the ones who didn't want to change in one cabin." Madelin looks at them suspiciously but brushes it off as we walk to the counter.

I can't unnotice their faces. They're literally red.

Interesting.

We all pay for what we picked. Dad left me and Alex money for food and bills even though Alex told me he usually works in the Summer but he has taken a few weeks off since I came and we're going on the vacations.

We exit the shop and walk around a little bit until I notice someone. He puts his arm over Madelin's shoulder.

"Hello, cousin." A voice says.

I look at the guy.

And he winks at me.

That guy. The one from the party.

AN: -word count- 1771

I don't know how to feel about this. I think my writing is rushed and I don't know how to describe emotions also everything happens so quickly.

Let me know if you agree.

Thank you so much for your support!

Byee<3

7

My mind freezes and I look away. But I don't stop walking. I can see him better now. His stare cuts through me.

But something else is on my mind.

Suddenly I'm back at that party. I feel his eyes on me. The way he looked at me and the hungry stare. The way he looked at my body.

And then when I came out of the bathroom. The way he touched me. And I felt so dirty. I can still feel his hand there.

It makes me sick.

But..

He's Madelin's cousin?

I come back to the present when cold air hits my face. We're back in the parking lot.

And they're gone.

And it's just me, Madelin, Mers and Ayna again.

Was I imagining them?

"Cade is so annoying. I can't stand him. And why is he coming on vacation with us?" Mers asks furiously.

"I told you the house is his as much as it is mine." Madelin says. "And he's obviously coming there just to annoy us. At least the house is big so we hopefully won't see him much."

"His friends will be there too. They're jerks." Ayna says.

Madelin now turns to me. "That was my cousin. He's a dick but you have obviously already noticed that."

I smile a bit but don't say anything.

It's dark and street lamps are lightening the parking lot.

We make our way to the car. We all sit in with Mers and Ayna in the back. I'm in the front and Madelin is driving.

"Wait Valeri, can we stay at yours?"

"Yessss that would be so cool." Mers says excitedly.

"I don't know. I'll have to ask Alex." I say.

"Alright call him."

I do as they say and take the phone from my bag and dial my brother.

He picks up after the first ring.

"Valeri."

"Hey-" I start but Mers takes the phone from my hand.

"Heyy Alex. Soo we wanted to ask if we can stay at yours."

Its quiet for a couple of seconds.

"Okay...alright...yeah we're heading back right know...no, no she didn't...
okay...so we can come?...they are?...that's even better...thanks...bye."

"We fucking love your brother." Mers says.

"Hell yeah." Ayna agrees.

She returns my phone and we soon pull into our driveway.

We all get out of the car and make our way up the stairs.

We see them in the backyard with a fire next to them. Alex, Zach, Kian and
Lachlan are sitting on the floor eating pizza.

Again?

Nevermind.

Lachlan jumps up and pulls me into a crashing hug. "I haven't seen you for
such a long time. I missed you." He says with a playing smile.

"You saw me yesterday."

"Too long."

I can literally feel everyone roll their eyes.

He pulls away and sits back down on the floor bringing me with him. He's
on my left and Zach is on my right.

Madelin, Mers and Ayna sit down as well.

"How was at Cade's?" Kian starts a conversation.

At the mention of his name my blood runs cold. I know he didn't do
anything serious to me but it still makes me shiver.

"It was so fucking boring. Listening to him all day plus his friends were there most of the time. He's here now." Madelin says with boredom in her voice.

"Are you cold?" I hear a voice from my right. "Here..." Zachary takes off his hoodie and brings it over my head. It's so comfy. Maybe I should steal from him too.

"He's here? And he was with you at the mall?" Kian questions.

"He just came to say hi or whatever. He's a dick. And his friends too."

"Why do we hate him so much?" I speak up warming myself with Zach's hoodie.

"He's an ass. That's everything you need to know. You should stay away from him."

But what if he doesn't stay away from me?

"Noted." I mutter. I pick up a slice of pizza but just because Alex was eyeing me.

I chew on it slowly as the conversation goes on.

I make it through with just one slice of pizza. I'm so hungry but I can't.

"Do you know what time it isssssss?" Lach yells.

Literally yells.

Everyone is silent and he acts as if he is fake hurt but then a smile lights up his face.

He gets up and runs into the house.

For fuck's sake.

He returns screaming a moment later."Marshmallows!"

He has two huge bags of them in his hand and he throws them at Kian.

"What the fuck do you have with me?" Kian says. I don't miss the way he tries to cover up his smile.

"You need to chill down man." Alex says.

"Marshmallows! I fucking love them!" Mers yells and opens the bag.

She and Lach fill their mouths with them.

Let's forget the fact that they're still raw.

"Fuch off give them to me." Ayna says and takes the bag.

After a decade of arguing we all sit around the fire.

I don't take any. I have never tried them.

"Miss Valeri why the fuck are you not eating marshmallows?" Lachlan points at me with his finger.

"You don't like them?" Zach says from beside me.

"I've never tried them. And I usually don't even it much sugar. Sweets and that." I shrug with my shoulders.

They're too sweet and I don't like that. Chocolate too except if it is dark.

"Don't say that, girl, you're putting yourself in danger." Madelin warns me.

After Lach finishes lecturing me, we all just lie down and stare at the sky. We decided we're going to sleep outside since we are too lazy to actually get up.

I'm laying on my back with Zach next to me. Ayna and Mers are a couple metres away seeming to have a good time.

I stare into the stars and just let the thoughts swim away. I still have Zach's hoodie on me. Oops a mistake. My hoodie now. I fucking love it. And it smells like him. I take a deep breath.

I try to sleep but I can't. The dark and what's in it pretty scares me.

I don't know how much time I just lie there but I can't do it anymore. And the thought of having a panic attack infront of everybody...

When I hear everyone is asleep I look at Zachary.

He's already looking at me though.

"Can't sleep?" He breaks the silence.

"Nah." I exhale.

"Are you scared of the dark?" He asks.

"Yup." My cheeks redden.

"But just when you're outside." He mumbles.

I almost don't hear him.

Wait how does he know?

"Do you want to go inside?"

"Yes. That'd be great." I let out a shaky breath.

Zach stands up and takes my hand to pull me up with him. I can feel how exhausted I am now so I can't help but lean into him. Why is he so familiar?

He puts his arm over my shoulder and we quietly walk over the backyard. The house is dark but we don't put the lights on since we don't want to wake others up.

I stumble at least three times until Zach picks me into his arms.

This is so weird.

I put my hands around his neck and he carries me into my bedroom.

Zach puts me down on my bed and I'm almost asleep by now.

As he's on his way to leave the room I stop him.

"Can you stay?" I feel safe with him.

He turns back to me looking for something on my face.

"Are you sure?" He asks.

"Yes." I whisper.

I'm half asleep when I feel a body lie down next to mine.

I close my eyes and drift off.

ZACHARY

Here she is. Right next to me. My favourite person but she doesn't know it.

I'm worried about her. She doesn't eat much. But she's doing so much better. Alex told me she didn't eat anything at the mall and she ate just one slice of pizza. I could see it on her face she felt sick. It's not much but it's something. And I am so proud of her.

I want to tell her so much. But I can't. I don't want to bring her back into the past. I don't want to lose her again. And I can help her either way, as I've already told Alex.

Now she's sleeping next to me. I don't know if she still gets panic attacks at night buy I'll be here for her if she has one.

I missed her so fucking much. It was killing me. I left her there alone and there wasn't a moment I didn't feel guilt in my heart.

I wish I could tell her how sorry I am. But it isn't the time yet.

VALERI

I wake up in the middle of the night again.

I have a hard time breathing as usual.

It happens every single night and I hate it. I haven't slept one whole night for years.

Knowing what's going to happen I get out of the bed and shut myself into the bathroom.

I am uncontrollably shaking by now and my hands are trembling as I open the drawer. I take my package of pills and shake them into my hand. I don't know how many of them there is because I'm losing my vision.

I sit down on the cold floor and put them into my mouth. I can feel hot tears streaming down my face.

I'm so scared. I'm so so scared.

It must be minutes but it could've been hours until painkillers kick in.

I slowly calm down.

As I'm trying to control my breathing I hear a soft knock on my bathroom door.

"Valeri? Are you okay? I'm coming in if you don't answer me."

Fuck. I completely forgot about Zach. I didn't even try to be quiet.

I convince myself he didn't hear me and clean my face.

He's standing infront of me as I open the bathroom door.

I quickly slip past him and lie back down in my bed. I don't want him to ask questions.

After a few seconds of silence I feel him lie down next to me.

"Are you okay?"

I let out a breath as if I just fell back to sleep. But I can feel someone is playing with my hair. I'm too tired to think about it. I just know it helps me calm down.

AN: -word count- 1767

That's the first chapter I actually love.

I love Valeri and Zach and Lach of course.

Before you read next chapters you should check trigger warnings again.

If you're struggling with your mental health please at least try to reach out for help!

I love y'all byee

8

The next morning I wake up with Zachary sleeping next to me. His dark hair is falling over his eyes as he breathes slowly. I sit up and look around. I hear others downstairs so it must be late.

Not wanting to wake Zach I quietly get out of bed. I take some clothes from my wardrobe and enter the bathroom. I still have his hoodie on me. The cold water wakes me up completely. After I change my clothes I put Zach's hoodie back on and go back into my bedroom again.

Zach is awake now and he's sitting on my bed.

This is so awkward.

"Morning." He says with his sleepy voice. He looks at my clothes and then smirks up at me.

"Hey." I softly say and return a grin.

"How are you?" Zach asks as he gets up and towers over me. He clears his throat.

"I'm great." Please get me out of here.

The others save me when we hear laughter coming from the kitchen.

"We should get downstairs." I quickly slip out of the room. I hear him follow me as I walk down the stairs.

We enter the kitchen together.

"We thought a bear ate you two." Mers laughs out.

Alex eyes me suspiciously and I feel ashamed. What was I thinking when I invited his best friend to sleep in my bed? It was nothing but still.

I sit next to Lach who is throwing strawberries in Ayna's mouth. Mers is hyping them up and Kian is rolling his eyes.

Interesting.

Madelin is chatting with Alex who's staring at me.

I sit down opposite him and hear a chair next to mine move. Zach sits down beside me.

"Valeri." My brother says. "You should pack your things."

"Hold up. Are you kicking her out?" Lach takes a step closer to me. "Are you kicking her out just because she was sleeping with Zachy? You can't blame her, man, I'd happily do that too."

Mers laughs out loud.

I give Lach a murder look and he jumps back.

"Shut up dude I'm not kicking her out. We're going on vacation tomorrow so we should all get ready. Same goes for you."

There's an uncomfortable silence.

"Ooooooh. My bad. I forgot." His cheeks turn red.

"So when are we going?" Zachary asks trying to change the subject.

I gratefully smile at him.

"Tomorrow morning. We need a few hours to get there." Madelin says.

They start going home one by one.

Zach makes me a toast and when I finally eat it it's just me he and Alex.

Zach seems to finally notice his best friend's wary look.

"It was nothing." Zach holds up his hands.

"I just couldn't sleep outdoors so we went inside. And I asked him to stay because I'm scared of the dark." I mumble the last part.

Alex lets out a sigh. "Alright I guess. I mean I have no say in what you two are doing."

After we finish our conversation I run up to my bedroom. I don't know what to do so I start packing my things. Alex gave me a suitcase.

My phone gets me out of my thoughts.

I pick it up.

THE HOTTEST BITCHES ALIVE

Ayna: 911! I have no idea which dress to take with me!*picture 1*picture 2

Mers: Take both so I can see which one is easier to take off.

W rizz

Madelin: I agree.Madelin: With the first part, ofc!

Ayna: Thanks Madelin<3Ayna: You're not helping Mers.Ayna: Valeri what do you think?

Me: I like the purple one better but you look good in both.

Ayna: I don't know. Can anyone please come at my place? Because it doesn't look good on camera.

Mers: I volunteer as tribute! I volunteer as tribute!

Madelin: I want to come too!!!

Ayna: You should all come. Valeri?

Me: I don't know. I'll ask Alex after I pack my stuff. Almost done.

Ayna: Alr! Come over when you can.

I put my phone away and put the last few things into my suitcase. When I'm done I go to my brother's room and knock.

"Come in."

Zach.

I open the door. They're both laying on the bed playing video games. It looks like they've already packed.

"Hey." I step in. "Can someone drive me to Ayna's?

"Did you pack?"

"Yup."

"Alright. Come on." Alex says getting up. "Give me two minutes." He closes the bathroom door after him so now it's just me and Zach here.

He stands up and walks over to me. He pulls me into his arms. I have no idea when did we get this close.

"Hey." He whispers in my ear.

"Hi." I look in his eyes.

"You look beautiful today." He whispers so Alex doesn't hear.

"I look beautiful everyday." I tease him back.

I know we are just joking but it just feels right.

Zach jumps back on the bed as we hear the bathroom door unlocking.

"Ready?" My brother says.

"Yup."

We go downstairs in a garage. Alex starts the car. It's just a few minutes drive.

"When should I pick you up?" Alex smiles at me.

"I'll call you."

Alex stops the car when we get there.

"I know I'm getting on your nerves but you should eat something at Ayna's, okay? Mers will definitely make pancakes. She always does them."

I look away.

"I'm sorry for bringing it up but I really care." He sadly smiles.

"I understand."

"Come here." He kisses my forehead. "See ya. And no alcohol."

We'll see.

I get out of the car and walk up the stairs to the door.

Mers opens the door with apron and a spatula. "Hello! Hello! Come in!"

Ayna comes running to the door. "Mers! I told you that you'll be the one cleaning the floor if you make a mess." She puts her hand around Mers' waist and softly pushes her back into the kitchen. "Hey, Valeri, come in."

I do as she says. As I enter the kitchen I see two bottles of vodka on the table and next to them there's a tower of pancakes. The walls are white and the cabinets are dark red.

Madelin comes crushing into me. "You need to spill the tea, girl. Come onnnnn. Sit down."

When we are all sitting around the table, Mers dramatically puts palms on it.

"So. We are playing Never have I ever while we eat pancakes. Whoever eats the pancake first loses or wins or whatever."

"We are not ten." Ayna rolls her eyes.

"Maybe you're not but you sure act like it." Mers winks at her.

"Bitch." Ayna says under her breath and shakes her head.

"Alright let's start." Madelin says. "Never have I ever hooked up with someone in exchange for alcohol."

She takes a bite of her pancake.

And then Mers.

And then me.

Oops.

We all look at Ayna.

"I'm not that much of a whore like you guys." She scoffs.

Mers laughs.

"Alright alright let's continue. Valeri."

What should I say? Okay I got it.

"Never have I ever had sex with the same gender." I say.

Now you can hear us all chewing.

I was not expecting that.

"You're gay too?" Mers looks at me expecting.

"Bi." I say.

"Oh my god me too!" Madelin hugs me.

"We can all tell you how we realised it later." Ayna says.

I smile at her. I've never told anyone.

"Never have I ever slept with Zachy." Mers says and now they all turn to me.

My cheeks heat up and I probably look like a tomato right now.

"Why are you all staring at me?" I cover my face.

"Because we found him in your bed this morning."

"It was nothing. I hate sleeping outside so he came inside with me. And yes I asked him to stay and he did."

They eye me suspiciously.

"I promise." I add.

"Okay girl but we all know something is going on between you two. I mean he obviously likes you." Madelin says.

"I agree." The other two girls add.

"But it would be weird. He's my brother's best friend. Alex told us he won't keep us apart but I feel kind of guilty because of last night." I tell them.

"Yeah we get it. But you should go for it."

"I don't even know if I like him. Plus I've never been in a relationship. At least not in healthy one." I shrug with my shoulders.

"Well don't push it. You'll know when you'll know." Mers gives me an advice.

"I guess."

~~~

I

t's been a few hours and of course we are all wasted. I fucking love it. Vodka is my life. We went swimming, we did ourselves face masks, we shared every detail of our love life. I love being a woman.

Mers and Ayna are passed out and me and Madelin are barely awake. That's when a ringing phone startles me.

Fuck. How long has it been?

I pick it up.

Madelin hits my arm meaning to say to act not wasted or whatever that means.

I click accept.

"Valeri, what the fuck are you doing?" I hear my brother's voice through the phone.

"Huh?"

Madelin hits my arm again.

"I'm sorry, what?" I correct myself.

"You're drunk."

"Nope. Never. Not even a little bit." I say.

"Okay, we are picking you up right now. Stay on the phone." Alex says.

And the dumbass I am I hang up.

Thousands of years later I hear the front door shut and heavy footsteps down the hallway.

I'm just there laying on a couch with a bottle of vodka in my hand.

The four of them enter the living room and Alex runs up to me and takes the bottle away.

"Hey don't be a duck." I stutter.

"Fucking hell Valeri. How much have you had?"

"Actually not that much."

"Okay." He sadly smiles. "Come on." Alex turns to someone and says something about them staying here with girls but I'm almost asleep.

I feel another cold hand stroking my cheek. "I got you, I got you, Val."

Val.

AN: -word count- 1701It'll start happening in the next or in two chapters so keep reading.

Check TWs if you haven't already.

If you're struggling with your mental health please, at least try to reach out for help!

What do you think about Valeri and Zach? What do you think about the story?

Please vote and COMMENT! I love reading them❤

9

My head is pounding and there's ringing in my ears.

It takes me a while until I open my eyes.

I'm lying in my bed. What the fuck happened?

"Valeri." I hear a voice from behind me.

I roll over..

My body aches and pain shots through my head.

"Are you okay?" Zach says. "Here." He holds up a glass of water. I sit up and take it from him. I swallow a few times and give it back to him.

"My head hurts. Really hurts." I put it between my hands. "What happened?"

"You got drunk as fuck." I hear my brother's voice as he enters the room.

"Oh. Where are the others?" I'm wondering what happened to Ayna, Mers and Madelin.

"They're still there. Lach and Kian are looking over them. But, Valeri, what were you thinking?"

"Can't we just get drunk?" I ask.

He shakes his head. "Come on. We need to get going."

"Where?" I'm so lost.

"Ohhh yeah I remember now."

I go in the bathroom and quickly change my clothes and brush my teeth because I smell of alcohol.

My head is hurting but it looks like I've run out of painkillers. Fuck.

I get out and they're still sitting on my bed.

"Do you have any painkillers?" They will hopefully give me more then one.

"Yeah but you'll have to eat something first."

I follow them out of my room down the stairs into the kitchen.

"I need to go check on the others and look if we're ready to go. You..." My brother points at me. "Need to eat something."

I nod.

Alex takes off and now it's just me and Zachary.

"What do you want to eat?" I hear him say."

"I don't know. Something." I shrug with my shoulders.

"Alright. Sit down."

I do as he says and put my head on the table. I actually drift off until Zach shakes me awake. "You'll sleep on the road, okay?"

I look infront if me. Waffles. And they smell so good. But I shouldn't.

"I don't really have an appetite." I say not looking at him.

"You don't get your painkillers if you don't at least try to eat." He tells me.

That does it. I pick up a waffle and bite into it. It tastes perfect.

I eat both of them and Zach finally gives me a painkiller.

Just one. And then he puts them back into a cupboard.

At least I know where they are.

I swallow it without water.

~~~

It has been an hour and we are finally getting in the car. Madelin, Ayna, Mers and Kian are already on the road. Me, Alex, Zach and Lach just sat in the car. Alex is driving and Lach literally got in a fight with Zach because he wanted to sit at the front so now it's me and Zach in the back.

I lean my head on the window and try to sleep but it's too uncomfortable.

Zach seeming to notice pulls me to him and I lean my head on his lap. This. This is better. "Thanks." I don't know why I say it.

While I'm trying to take a nap I feel him stroking my long hair.

~~~

I wake up when Alex slows the car down. It looks like we arrived. Zach is still stroking my hair so I pretend to be asleep for a little while.

"I know you're awake." Zach says from above.

"No, I'm not." I mumble.

"We're here, you slept for twelve hours today. I can't believe you're still tired."

I grin and sit up. I have to blink a few times because of the light.

"Everyone is already inside. Come on." He takes my hand and we get out.

There's a house infront of us. It has a pool and really big windows. It faces the sea that's behind us. It's beautiful here.

Zach takes mine and his luggage and we head up.

We can already hear Lach and Mers screaming at each other as he tries to throw her in a pool.

Yup. They are doing just that.

"Valeri please help! Please! No Lach! Fuck off! Put me down!" Mers yells. Ayna is cheering.

Fuck. I completely forgot about swimming. What the fuck am I supposed to do? How did I forget about it?

"Lach is such a kid." Zach shakes his head but I notice his smile-his dimples.

Cute.

He puts a hand around my shoulder and we enter the house. His touch calms me and that's probably why I love being in his presence.

There's a kitchen and a huge living room that has a view on the sea. There's a couch and a TV.

We leave our suitcases in here and go back out to the pool. It looks like Lach reached what he wanted since Mers is in the pool with her wet clothes. But I don't think that was enough. He's sneaking up behind Madelin and Ayna and in a second they're both in the water.

I think we all know who the next target is.

Shit. Lach picks me up over his shoulder even if I protest.

"Put me down you piece of shit."

But he does not listen. I can't help but laugh.

And suddenly I'm in the air and then the cold water hits my body.

I come back on the surface. "Have you ever even considered that maybe I can't swim?" I yell at him.

"Nope I mean who can't swim?" He jumps in the pool after us.

Jerk.

~~~

Alex brought some towels to dry off. We are all just chilling outside when we hear a car pull in the driveway.

"Fuck. Cade is here." Madelin stops the conversation.

Cade.

I forgot about him.

A group of people comes up the stairs. There's some guys including Cade and two girls.

"What the hell are you doing here?" Madelin asks her cousin.

"I heard there's a huge party later tonight." He smirks at her. "Don't act surprised, you knew we were coming."

As he looks around his eyes lock with mine. I shift uncomfortably.

He waves at the others to follow him inside but before the door close I can feel his stare on me.

"I'm so sorry he's here." Madelin says.

"No it's okay. Though I really hate him and his friends." Alex sighs.

~~~CHECK TWs! If it's too hard for you to read you can skip this part!

It's getting dark and there's so many people already. It seems like Cade has invited some of his other friends.

I don't know anyone so I stick to Alex. He warned me to not accept a drink from anyone but of course I already knew that. He also said that I shouldn't drink as much as yesterday but it feels so good. It's like my thoughts die.

I'm dancing with Madelin now. I can see Mers and Ayna grinding against each other.

I drank a little so I feel a bit dizzy but it's nothing compared to yesterday.

Suddenly I feel like I need some air so I leave Madelin's side. I go to the opened front door and sit down near the pool. There's not much people here. Most of them are inside.

Alcohol is making me lightheaded and my low iron helps him.

Someone sits down next to me.

It's dark so I can't really see who it is but I can feel it's a guy.

I notice he's smoking weed. Now I want some too.

It looks like he notices because he holds it up to me. "Want some?"

I know I shouldn't but fuck it. I take it from his hand and inhale. My nerves immediately calm down. My brother is going to kill me if he finds out. I take a few more drags and now my mind is finally quiet. I lean against that guy's shoulder and he puts a hand around my waist stroking my hip. I shift a little.

He pulls me up and drags me inside. I don't think I feel safe anymore but my head is empty. I protest when he pushes me up the stairs but he keeps me quiet with his palm over my mouth.

We are upstairs now. He holds my wrists and I try to fight him but I can't. He pushes me in a room and follows me inside.

I can see him now. He's one of Cade's friends. As if Cade hears my thoughts he enters the room.

They both move closer and I step back until my knees hit the bed.

No. No. Please.

Cade closes the space between us as he strokes my cheek. "Valeri." He whispers.

"No please don't."

"Don't what?" He says as he pushes me back on the bed.

I quickly get up but his friend is there too. He takes me into his arms and pushes me back down.

They both tower over me.

"Please don't." I beg as Cade lifts up my dress. I hit his hand but it doesn't help.

"Don't make a sound or it'll be so much worse." He threatens.

I have to find Alex or Zach. Anyone.

I know what's about to happen so I do the only thing Cade told me not to do.

I yell for Alex.

I immediately regret it as his hand finds its way to my face.

I don't hear anything. And I can't say anything because his friend's palm is now covering my mouth.

I can hear someone unbuckling his belt but I keep my eyes shut.

"You're doing great, baby. Don't move." I can feel him now. His hot breath is on my cheek and I feel like throwing up.

I feel him thrust inside and tears sting my eyes. I try to push him off but someone is holding my legs and I know their hands will leave bruises.

He's rough. I can't fight anymore so I just lie there staring at the door with hope that someone will come looking for me.

But no one does.

I try to quiet my moans but my body does otherwise.

A loud sob leaves my mouth and a hand finds a way to my face again. Pain consumes my whole body and I can't move anymore.

Cade pulls out and I'm full of hope that this is over but no.

I lie there staring at the ceiling as his friend finds me. He turns me around so I'm on my stomach now. I feel his breath on my neck and I bury my face in the pillow. This is not happening. Please.

He pulls me up on my knees with my face still in the sheets.

"Be quiet you whore." I hear him say as he thrusts into me. Pain consumes my body once again.

I keep myself distracted with counting. I count until he finishes and pulls his pants back up and I just lie there until I hear the door shut after them.

AN: -page count- 1821This was really hard to write knowing too many people are going through it but I want to raise awareness.

If you struggle with anything like this please try to reach out for help.

I love you all so much and please know there's someone out there who will listen to you❤

10

Check TWs if you're about to read this chapter.

What has just happened?

I feel empty even though my whole body hurts. I feel empty even though I'm covered in bruises. I feel empty even though I feel blood dripping out of my nose on the pillow.

I want to lie here forever and just die. I want it to end. I want it all to end.

After I process what happened I try to get up. My body aches and there's blood all over my thighs.

I look around and realise I'm in my room.

I get off of the bed and stumble to the door. My vision goes black for a few seconds and I almost pass out.

I quickly lock the door. I don't want anyone to find me here. I don't want anyone to ever know.

My hands are shaking and I feel cold.

I fall onto my knees as I search for clothes. I can't keep myself up.

I slowly walk in the bathroom with my hand on the wall trying to keep myself standing.

As soon as I enter I fall over and throw up in the toilet.

My breaths are heavy and I feel the panic flood me. No not now. I need to clean everything up and I don't have my painkillers.

I lean my head on the wall behind me and try to calm myself down. You're okay Valeri. You're okay.

But am I?

I survive the panic attack like every night and as it ends I just sit there for I don't know how long.

I can see them every time I close my eyes. I can feel them touching me where I didn't want to.

I get up throw the clothes off of me and go in the shower and put the water as hot as it can go. It's burning my skin hopefully deleting all traces of them. But I know that's not possible.

I can clean the blood but I can't clean their touch. I rub my arms and thighs as hard as I can but the cold of their hands stays there.

I feel dirty. I feel like my body isn't mine anymore and I can't imagine looking at myself in the mirror. I don't want to see my bruised cheeks. I don't want to see my bleeding nose. I don't want to see my body that isn't really mine anymore.

How could I let it happen? Did I want it? I know my body liked it. But my mind didn't. What does that mean? Did they really do something wrong?

I don't want to look down. I don't want to look at my body because I know what I'm going to see.

I turn the water off and step out. Now I can't avoid the mirror.

I'm staring in my unrecognisable body. The bruises are getting bigger and bigger. There are red lines on both of my wrists.

I look at my face. My cheek is swollen and red. I know it will be blue by tomorrow.

What the fuck am I supposed to do? I can't stay in my room for the rest of the week or even more.

And how am I supposed to hide everything when we go swimming? Should I find Alex or Zach or anyone?

But I can't face Madelin. I just can't. I know she didn't do anything wrong but knowing that her cousin was in my room tonight...

What if they come back? What if this will continue?

I open the drawer under the sink and find a gauze. I clean up the cuts that were probably made by their fingernails.

I'm relieved when I realise I'm not bleeding from my private places. I know I'm supposed to tell someone and go to the gynecologist but I can't do that right now.

I put on some clean underwear, sweats and a t-shirt. That's when I notice my dress on the floor. There's some blood on it but not much. Just a look at it causes flashbacks.

Should I put it somewhere if I will need the evidence? I know I shouldn't have showered either.

I find a bag and put the dress and dirty underwear in it. As I enter the bedroom I don't really look, I just pull off the sheets and put them in the bag as well.

Pain shoots through my body as I push everything under the bed.

I don't feel safe and the t-shirt that I'm wearing is not helping either.

After going through my clothes I finally find Zach's hoodie and quickly slip it on. It feels like home.

A knock on the door startles me.

Fuck.

What if it's them again? What if they came back? I shiver.

"Valeri?" I flinch at my name. It's Zach.

"Yeah?" I'm surprised when I hear my voice is steady.

"Where were you? Can I come in?" He asks.

"Give me a second I don't feel good." I run to the bathroom and put out all my make up. I put on a concealer as fast as I can but I can't cover up my swollen cheek.

Fuck. I'll find some excuse.

I check if I'm covered and then I go back into my room. I close the lights and unlock the door.

Zach is still waiting outside. "Where were you? You just disappeared." He says worriedly. He checks my face and...

Fuck. He can see it can't he?

He brings his hand up to my cheek and I flinch back. "What happened?"

"I think I might have drunk too much and I kind of crashed in a wall." I say the first thing that comes in my mind.

"You aren't drunk anymore?" He searches my face.

"Maybe I am." I shrug with my shoulders.

That's when I hear the house is silent. How long ago had it happened?

"Is everyone gone?" I ask.

"Yeah, we couldn't find you so we called it off."

"Oh." I look down. "Well, I'm going back to sleep if you let me."

"Alright." He gently hugs me. His touch isn't like theirs.

I squeeze him back even if my body tells me otherwise. Zach makes me feel safe.

I quickly pull away. "Night." I mutter.

"I'm in the room next to yours if you need anything."

"Okay."

"Night, Valeri."

I close the door and lean back on it. I hear him walk away but I wish he had stayed.

I finally free my tears. I feel like there's a knot in my throat that tries to keep me from breaking down but my pain wins over. I fall down on the floor as I sob in my hands.

What if they come back? A thought that they're in the same house as me makes me even more scared.

How could I let it happen?

The pain is overwhelming and I really need something. Anything.

But I don't have painkillers.

And I know I shouldn't.

I stop crying because of the fight in my head. It's getting louder.

Should I? Shouldn't I?

I stand up on shaking legs and freeze.

Should I? Shouldn't I?

I literally just stand in the middle of my room. My head is empty.

Should I?

I walk into the bathroom telling myself I'll just drink some water but as soon as I see a razor blade...

Should I?

I've been clean for more then two months but the pain in my mind doesn't stop.

I take a deep breath.

You know what? We will all die one day. Does it really matter?

I pick it up and sit down by the door.

It heals too soon if I do it on my wrist.

I pull down my pants and see my bruises.

Why does what they did to me hurt so much?

The voices in my head are becoming louder and louder and a sob leaves my mouth.

Am I really going to relapse after doing so great?

I can feel the blade on my thigh now. I go slowly at first. I don't look. My eyes are closed. I pull it across my skin and feel a burning pain. I want to yell out but nothing comes out of my throat. I do it again faster. I feel the cut open and I look down just as it turns red.

My mind is quiet now. It feels like there's no time.

I do it again and again and again. Pain shoots through my leg.

Why is this so satisfying? Feeling the burning sensation and seeing it turn red? Seeing how blood pours out of it down my leg? I sob into my hand with the other one still holding the weapon.

Is this it? Did I just relapse? I thought I could finally fit in. I was actually feeling happy. I have friends and a brother who cares about me? And I still do it?

It's just the way I cope. It's not always to quiet down my thoughts. Sometimes I just feel the need to see my blood. That I'm actually real.

I just sit here watching blood dripping down my leg.

What have I just done? What the fuck.

Guilt. I feel guilt now.

Regret.

How am I going to cover this up?

I pull my pants off and stand up. As soon as I put the weight on my leg I almost fall down but I catch myself.

There's so much blood. So much.

I clean it up with some paper towels and then let the cuts breathe a bit. After a few minutes I wrap my thigh with a bandage.

Did I go too far?

I clean the blood on the floor and pull my sweats up when I'm done.

I don't want to be alone right now. I don't feel safe. I need someone.

I go in my room and look at my bed.

"You're doing great, baby. Don't move."

"Be quiet you whore."

I go to the door, unlock and open it. I listen for a few seconds and then slip out. I turn right and knock on the first door.

It opens and Zach's figure is standing infront of me.

I wish I could open the door like that. Without a second thought.

"Valeri? What are you doing here?" He whispers as he moves back so I can come in.

"I don't feel great. My head is pounding." I say as he closes the door behind us.

"Come here." He says and puts a hand on my forehead.

I flinch a little but let him touch it.

"You're burning up."

Wait really? Great.

"You want to stay here?" He asks worriedly.

"If you don't mind." I mutter.

"No, no just get on the bed. I'll bring you a glass of water." He says and goes in the bathroom.

Only the light on his bedside table is on so it's pretty dark in here. I sit down on the bed. My head is killing me.

He returns a minute later with water and pills.

Pills.

"Here. If your head hurts too much." He says as he sits next to me.

I swallow it and put the empty glass on the nightstand.

"Is it okay if I sleep next to you? I don't want to make you uncomfortable." Zach asks.

It sounds unreal.

"No, that's okay. It's your bed."

He smiles at me and I want to do the same but I can't.

"Okay then. Good night Valeri." He says as he gets into bed beside me.

I pull a sheet over me and close my eyes.

"Is it okay if I close the light?"

"Yeah." I don't want him to see me.

A second later I hear a click and the darkness overcomes the room.

It's so cold. Why is it so cold? I can't help but shiver. And I can't stop.

I feel Zachary put hands around me and pull me close to him. I'm in his arms now. I'm safe.

"Good night, Zach." I say as I close my eyes.

AN: -word count- 2007This chapter was really hard for me to write because I struggle with self harm myself.If you're struggling with your mental health please try and reach out for help. There's always someone who cares enough to listen.I love you❤bye

----

11

Z ACHARY

It's already noon and Valeri is still sleeping. Probably because of the fever. But it doesn't stop her from looking as gorgeous as always.

The others woke up hours ago and they're currently swimming and having fun. I feel bad for Valeri. I know she has been on vacations only a few times. Always with me. I actually taught her how to swim since her mother never has.

And now she's sick. She will hopefully get better in a few days but still. Alex is really worried about her. He knows about everything Valeri was dealing in the past. I've told him before he even found out he has a twin sister. I have told him everything about her. How funny and nice she is. How she always puts others first before herself. How she is the most amazing person I have ever met.

I wish I could tell her how much I missed her but I know I can't. She's so much happier now. Plus we are getting pretty close so it doesn't really matter that much.

I read a book until she finally stirs awake. I put the book away and go in the bathroom to bring her a glass of water.

As I come back she's sitting on my bed looking confused.

"Finally awake? It's noon." I smile at her. But she doesn't do the same. I brush it off with a thought that she isn't feeling great since she's sick.

"Hey." She drinks the whole glass.

I put my hand on her forehead hoping she's not heating as much as she was last night.

She isn't. Good. But she looks really tired. Her face is pale and she has dark circles under her eyes.

"How are you feeling?" I ask because she doesn't say anything.

"Drained." Her voice is so soft. I love listening to her.

"I'll bring you something to eat, okay?" I pull her close.

"Okay."

I go downstairs and make her fresh orange juice and the pancakes that were left from breakfast. Lach only ate two just so Valeri could have more. That was so sweet of him.

I go back upstairs to my room but it's empty. I hear her in the bathroom so I wait for her.

She comes out a minute later looking a little bit better but she's still pale.

As soon as she sees me she starts apologising. "I'm sorry I didn't ask you to use your bathroom I just..."

"No it's okay it really isn't a problem."

"Oh okay." She doesn't meet my eyes. She hasn't since I saw her at the party.

Valeri sits back on the bed covering herself with a blanket. Covering her hoodie. I mean my hoodie. She still hasn't returned it and I don't expect her to.

I give her the plate with food. I can see she hasn't eaten anything for quite a long time.

Seeing her struggle breaks my heart. She's perfect but she doesn't see it.

"You don't have to eat everything if you don't want to, okay? Just try." I say quietly as I stroke her hair.

"I want to. I really do. But I can't." She whispers still looking at the pancakes. As I feel her start sweating and breathe faster I know what's going to happen. She tries to hide it but I've already noticed.

I put the plate away. "Hey hey, Valeri. Look at me, gorgeous." I can't help but use the nickname with which I used to call her a few years ago.

She's shaking in my arms by now. "It's okay. I'm here." I whisper.

It gets worse. I see tears streaming down her face.

"I've got you. Focus on me. Valeri, gorgeous. Look at me." She finally does.

Valeri stares in my eyes as she tries to breathe. "I'm scared. I'm so scared Zach."

The words do it. I pull her in my arms with her head on my chest. "It's okay, sweetheart. Breathe with me. Shhhhh." I stroke her hair.

It takes her a few minutes to calm down. She's breathing with a normal speed now and she looks exhausted. I haven't seen her so drained before. It makes me worry. Is this all because of food? Or are there other things? She has always had problems with eating but it wasn't this bad.

VALERI

I'm safe. I'm okay. I keep telling myself that but I know I'm lying. I don't know if I can keep what happened last night to myself for much longer. I should tell someone. I need to tell someone.

I'm so stupid. I've just had a panic attack infront of Zachary. What if he questions it? I should've known better.

I pull away from him and look away. I can't look him in the eyes. It's embarrassing. What if he will see me differently now?

I focus on my breathing.

I have to do better. I can't let him see me like this. He can't find out. I have to keep a distance. We got too close. From now on I will keep myself from him.

"Valeri." He reaches for my hand but I pull away and get up. My vision goes black for a few seconds and as I come back he's standing beside me. "Talk to me, Valeri. I want to help."

"I'm so sorry but you can't. It's too late. I need to be alone right now." I still don't look at him.

He catches my hand when I head to the door and I look up at him.

"You can always talk to me. I will listen, alright? I'll be here if you need me." He says worriedly.

I nod and exit. I get back in my room. The secret will be buried with me.

I get down on my knees and reach for the bag. I pull out the dirty sheets.

"Be quiet you whore."

I shake my head and take them to the bathroom. I open the washing machine and throw them in.

Is this a mistake?

I leave the clothes inside and push the bag back under.

I take new sheets from my wardrobe and put them on the bed. I lie down and cover myself with them.

"You're doing great, baby. Don't move."

I want to forget. I want to forget so bad. The flashbacks don't stop.

I get up and leave the room. I go downstairs to the kitchen. There have to be painkillers somewhere. If I ask Zach he will give me just one. It isn't worth it. I have to keep the distance even if my heart tells me otherwise.

I open every cabinet and finally find some. I check the date. They're a year old. I take them anyway and head back up in my room. I lock the door and sit back down on the bed. I have no idea if they'll help but I take some.

I lie down and wait to see if they will kick in.

Maybe because I took too much or maybe because they're old but I feel my breaths slow down. My eyes start closing and my head is empty. There's just silence. I forget about everything as I drift away.

~~~

Am I dead?

It sure feels like it.

I don't feel anything. Literally anything. All the pain is gone.

Good.

~~~

I wake up in sweat. This is the first time I slept without nightmares or waking up and having a panic attack.

Wow. It felt amazing. It felt so peaceful.

My head is still pounding though. I sit up even though my whole body aches.

Carefully I get out of the bed. Everything is spinning. Holy shit.

I enter the bathroom an splash some cold water on my face. It wakes me up completely.

I hear others downstairs. It seems like they're having fun.

Why can't I be like them?

As I come back in the bedroom I realise it's dark outside. It looks like I've slept for hours.

There's a knock on my door. Are they back?

I check myself in the mirror and open the door. Alex is standing infront of me. "Hey, I just wanted to check up on you. Zach told us you are sick. I came here a few times but you didn't respond." He sadly smiles.

My head is empty. There's nothing there.

"Oh. I was sleeping. Sorry." I say quickly.

"You don't look the best. Are you sure you're okay?" He asks.

"Yeah I'm fine." I shrug with my shoulders. "Where are others?"

"Downstairs. They were all so sad when they heard you're sick. I told them to not bother you."

"Thanks." I think for a few seconds. "Are Madelin's cousin and his friends still here?" I can't bring myself to say his name.

"Yeah but they're out right now."

I slowly nod.

AN: -word count- 1475Oh my god. We are on almost 300 reads! Thank you all so much for reading❤

If there are writing mistakes in this chapter just ignore them. It's almost 2am so...

What do you think? Will Valeri tell someone or will she keep everything to herself?

If you're struggling with mental health please try to reach our for help.(let's forget the fact that I never did.)

I love u all! Byee

12

It has been two days. I've spent most of the time sleeping in my room. I'm not feeling any better. At least not mentally. I don't have fever anymore even though I tell others I still do, so they let me be in my room.

I didn't have any panic attacks. Thanks to the pills. I was high most of the time. They help me keep my mind off things.

I cut myself more often. It just makes me feel better even though I feel like shit after I realise what I have done.

Alex and Zach came in my room a few times. Lach and the others too. But I pretended I was sleeping. They left some food. I ate enough to keep myself alive but flushed other down the toilet.

A knock on my door wakes me up and I sit up confused. How many did I take?

I get to the door and open it.

My brother.

He looks worried. "Are you still sick?"

"I don't know. Probably." I say. I think I took to many painkillers.

Alex puts a hand on my forehead. "Nope. Get downstairs. You slept for five days straight."

Five days?!

"Five?" I ask confused. Yup I've taken too much.

"Yeah."

"Alright."

"What's alright? Valeri." He looks at me with furrowed eyebrows.

"Oh nothing. Why are you here?"

"We're going to the beach if you want to come."

Beach? Fuck.

"Okay but I won't swim." I say slowly.

"Why not?"

"My head still hurts a bit."

"Oh okay I'll see you downstairs."

I change my clothes. I don't even bother looking at myself in the mirror because I know what I'm going to see. The bruises aren't getting any better.

I put on some sweatpants and a plain tee-shirt. I make sure the cuts are invisible to others.

As I'm done I get downstairs where Alex is waiting for me.

I get to him without saying anything. My head hurts and my legs are aching because of the scars on my thighs. I just want to go back to sleep.

I follow him outside and down to the beach. I can hear the others having fun. I wish I could have fun too.

At least it isn't that hot outside though it is warm enough to wear shorts.

"How are you feeling?" My brother asks me.

"Tired." I say. "And my head hurts as fuck."

"Have you already taken painkillers?"

"No." I lie.

He opens his bag pocket and takes out pills. He puts one in my hand. "Here."

This was easier than I thought.

I take it from Alex's hand and swallow it. "Thanks."

I don't know if this was a good idea since I probably still have the other ones in my system but fuck it.

We finally spot others. They're all in the water and I can see Lach is drowning Mers.

We put the towels on the sand. It's quite windy.

"Will you be here?"

"Yup." I sit down.

Alex walks up to the water and joins others. I lie down and close my eyes.

~~~

Someone shakes me awake.

"What the fuck Valeri? Valeri?" I open my eyes and roll on my back.

"Huh?"

"Are you even alive anymore?" My brother asks.

I sit up and pull my hand through my hair. "What? Yeah. Yeah I am." I look up.

Zachary is looking at me with worry in his eyes.

I look around. Everyone is taking their things. It must have been hours.

I stand up. "Valeri!!" Lach comes to hug me. "I haven't seen you in days." He squeezes me tightly and I almost pass out from the pain.

"You just disappeared for almost a week." Madelin says and gives me a hug.

Then we go back to the house.

It's getting dark. We sit down on the couch and Lach, Mers and Ayna make pancakes. Yup. Again.

I'm sitting next to Zachary. I feel bad for just leaving his room five days ago. He just isn't supposed to know. I really want to talk and spend time with him but I keep telling myself I should not.

ZACHARY:

I'm sitting next to Valeri. She covered herself with a blanket even though it's Summer. I wish she didn't leave my room five days ago because I wanted to talk to her about the panic attack. I feel the distance between us now and I don't like it. What had me worried was her sleeping for days. It was like she disappeared.

And today at the beach. She slept for another three hours and when she woke up she looked really confused.

Maybe it's nothing and I'm overreacting but I also assume she didn't eat most of the food we brought to her room. She's pale and can't keep up with the conversation we're having.

Valeri's right leg is bouncing and she's biting her lip. She probably doesn't realise what she's doing. I can see that she's really anxious about something. She keeps looking at the door like she is waiting for someone to walk in.

I lock my hand with Valeri's under the blanket. She looks at me and back to the door.

"What's wrong?" I whisper.

"Nothing." She quickly says and looks away so I can't see her face.

"Okay." I say slowly. I don't believe her. "Can I talk to you later?" I want to talk about the panic attack. If she won't want to talk about it I won't push her. I don't want to make her uncomfortable.

"What about?" Valeri asks.

"You know what."

"Okay I guess." She seems unsure.

"You don't have to talk about that if you don't want to."

She nods.

We hear the front door slam shut and voices on the hallway.

Valeri squeezes my hand tighter.

VALERI:

Cade and his friends enter the living room but they luckily don't stop and just go to the stairs.

But he still looks at me. Both of them do.

"Be quiet, you whore."

~~~

I

t's late. I have washed my hair since I didn't wash it for almost a week, I've brushed my teeth and I've changed in clean clothes. I put on Zach's hoodie and open the door of my room.

I know I told myself I should distance myself from him but he's the only person I feel like I can really talk to.

So here I am.

Sneaking in his bedroom.

Zach opens the door the moment I knock. It looks like he's just gotten out of the shower because his hair is wet. He is wearing grey sweats and a black tee-shirt. Why does he always look this fucking good?

He lets me in and closes the door.

"Hey." He smiles.

"Hi." I sit down on his bed.

"You still have my hoodie." He says.

"Do you want it back?" I ask.

"Nah, it looks better on you anyways." He smirks and I feel my cheek turning red. Luckily only his lamp is on.

Zach walks over to me and sits down. We get comfortable on his bed.

"Do you want to talk?" He asks while he's playing with my hair.

Do I?

"Okay." I look away.

"If you get uncomfortable just tell me okay?"

"Okay."

He sadly smiles at me.

We're both quiet for some time. "Does it happen often?"

Yup. Every night. Except for the past week because I was high as shit.

I leave out the last part. "Yeah. Every night. Sometimes through the day too." I try to blink the tears away. Why am I so emotional?

"Come here." Zach pulls me closer to him so I can lean my head on his chest.

"You can always come here when you need someone. It doesn't matter if it's four in the morning or four in the afternoon." He whispers and I nod.

"And I can't eat." Have I just said that? I'm surprised by the words that leave my mouth.

"I know. I've noticed. And Alex is worried too. Sometimes he wakes me up when he can't sleep because he's so worried." Zach's words cut right through me.

"Really?" I lift my head and look in his green eyes. I've never wanted to bother anyone. Especially my brother.

"Don't feel bad." He gives me a sad smile and tries to stroke my cheek.

I flinch back and quickly try to cover it by putting my head back on his chest.

I listen to his heartbeat. It calms me down. "I didn't mean to-"

"Can you tell him that I'm okay?" I mutter in his tee-shirt.

"Don't say that you're fine when you're not. Don't lie to yourself. Don't do this."

"I don't know what to do." I say. I'm talking about what happened but he doesn't know that.

"What do you mean?"

I sit up and pull my fingers through my hair. "Nothing. Forget it. I should go back to my room." I stand up.

"Did I do something wrong?" Zach says worriedly as he gets up.

"No. You did nothing wrong. I just need some time alone." I sigh.

"Alright." He pulls me in his arms. "If you need anything just come here. If you can't, just call me. You have my number." He kisses my forehead. I nod and step on the hallway.

I move towards my room and notice the door is a bit opened. I remember I closed it. I'm sure of it.

I slowly open it and turn the lights on. There's no one here. I look at my bed.

A piece of paper is on it.

I slowly step closer and pick it up with my fingers. I open it and read.

No.

This can't be happening.

I fall down on my knees and look under the bed.

There's nothing there.

Nothing.

AN: -word count- 1636Thank you all so much for all the nice comments<3We're on more than 400 reads! I've never imagined I would get this far. I started writing this book for myself only to prove I can do it but now I'm so happy other people like it too!

If you're struggling with your mental health please try to reach out for help!

Love uu

13

I stand there in shock. My mind is frozen in place.

He was in my room. Both of them were.

And they took the clothes I was wearing. This couldn't be happening. I have been gone for only around fifteen minutes.

As soon as I feel panic rising inside of me I run to the door and lock it. I take the pills from the drawer and lie down in the middle of the room.

They were in here.

I stare at the ceiling and when everything becomes too much I swallow some pills. I have no idea how much I take but they seem to help me. I calm down after a few minutes and just sob.

Why me? Why always me?

Loud sobs leave my mouth as I try to cover it with my hand. Tears are running down my cheeks not seeming to stop.

I feel alone. I feel so alone. I have to tell someone. I know I should but maybe if I keep it to myself I can forget it and act like it never happened.

They raped me.

The thought is stabbing my chest. My heart. My soul.

They raped me. They got what they wanted but they're still here. Right now they're in the same building as me. They can walk through my bedroom door anytime and I know I won't be able to stop them.

What if they come back?

What am I supposed to do?

I look at the pills. If I take too much maybe...

But I'm not going to do it.

It's just a thought.

ZACHARY

I know something is wrong. With Valeri. Something has happened. She has looked full of joy and happiness for a week and then just switched.

I lie in my bed for some time. I want to ask her if something has happened. Maybe I'm overreacting. Maybe it's just one of her depressive episode. She used to get them often and I always helped when she had one. I helped her showering. I made her food and I held her when she had nightmares or panic attacks.

I think Valeri needs my help.

Fuck I'm probably overreacting but I really need to make sure she's okay. My intuition is telling me that something is seriously wrong.

She flinched when I tried to touch her face. Did she think I was going to hit her?

That thought cuts right through my chest.

Alright I just need to see if she's okay.

I get off the bed and open my bedroom door. The hallway is dark but I can see a light coming from Valeri's room next to mine. It looks like she's still awake.

I come closer and listen. I don't want to wake her up if she's sleeping.

I hear something. Crying.

Wait is Valeri crying?

Shit.

I softly knock on her door and the noise immediately stops. But she doesn't open the door.

I listen for some time but I don't hear anything.

I try the doorknob but it looks like she locked it.

"Valeri? Open up." I knock again. "Please, gorgeous." But she doesn't do it.

"I'll wait out here until you come out." I sit down on the floor.

Time goes by and Valeri still doesn't open the door so I quickly get to my room and take a blanket and a pillow and come back on the hall.

I put everything on the floor infront of her room and lie down.

I hear only silence and fall asleep.

VALERI

I hear a knock on my door and immediately sit up.

Are they back? Will they touch me again?

Someone tries to open the door and I take a knife I stole from the kitchen.

"Valeri. Open up. Please, gorgeous." I exhale. It's Zach. Did he hear me crying? Was I too loud? Why is he here? I don't want to talk to him at the moment. I just want to be alone.

"I'll wait out here until you come out." I hear him sit down.

Should I open the door? Should I tell him?

No. It would make things worse.

I hear him stand up and walk away.

I sigh. Finally.

Zach is back not a minute later. I hear him throw something on the floor. He's probably lying down.

I step closer to the door and sit down. His soft breathing helps me calm down and drift off.

~~~

I wake up in sweat and sit up. Another bad dream. It's light outside but it must still be early. My legs and back are aching because of the position I slept in. The floor isn't really comfortable for sleeping. I look down and notice red on Zach's hoodie's sleeve.

Fuck. I forgot to clean them up yesterday.

I get off the floor as quickly as I can-really slow because my whole body hurts-and get in the bathroom. I turn on the shower and undress.

I take off Zach's hoodie and look at my wrist. I must have gone too deep because the cuts are still bleeding.

I take off my bra and pants until I'm standing naked infront of the mirror. The bruises are coloring my skin, my stomach and hips. My thighs are covered with dark red cuts. Some of them are a few years old but most of them are fresh.

What did I do? What did I do to my body? Myself?

I step in the shower and sit down. I feel burning as hot water pours on my thighs and wrists. It hurts so good. Warm water makes my cuts bleed even more. Blood Is dripping out of them and water washes it away leaving red lines.

When I step out of the shower I realise I went too far last night. And I was taking a hot shower now which made it even worse.

Shit shit shit.

The blood is slowly dripping down my arms and legs as I try to stop it. I usually just leave it to dry and then clean it up but that doesn't work now.

What the fuck did I do?!

I wipe the scars with a cold water and it gets better after a few minutes. I bandage everything up-my wrists and my thighs- and look in my reflection. I don't recognise the person infront of me. I haven't since it happened. The bruises are dark and aren't getting any better. My eyes are empty. I feel empty inside too.

I put on some clothes with long sleeves. I know it's hot as fuck outside but there's no other way. I brush my teeth and my face and get out leaving the door open because it's at least 30 degrees in there.

I unlock the door and see Zachary lying on the floor. I completely forgot about that.

Not wanting to wake him up I step back inside and lie down on my bed.

Losing blood made me tired and darkness takes me away again.

ZACHARY

"What the fuck are you doing infront of my sister's room?" Alex's voice wakes me up.

"Huh?" I mutter.

He slaps me across my face and I'm right awake. "Wake up dickhead."

I look up at him.

"Why are you sleeping on the hallway beside Valeri's door?" Alex asks.

"I don't know." I mumble. The memories of last night come back.

"Come on man let's go downstairs and eat lunch." He helps me up and we head down. It's already 12pm and Kian made lunch.

Lach and the girls join us while we are eating. It's already 1pm by then.

"Did anyone see Valeri today?" I thought she would be awake by now.

"Nope." No one saw her.

"You were the one sleeping infront of her room." My best friend says.

"Wait what?" Everyone asks but I quickly get up because I need to check if Valeri's okay. I run up the stairs until I come to her door. I knock.

She doesn't answer.

I knock a little louder.

Nothing.

I try her doorknob again and it surprisingly works. "Valeri?" I ask for her before I open the door wider.

I look around the room and see her on the bed. I come closer. She's sleeping. "Valeri? It's late." I shake her by her shoulder.

She doesn't move.

I shake her harder.

First nothing and then she quickly sits up breathing hard.

"Val?"

"Zach. You fucking scared me." She looks at me. "What are you doing here?" She gets off the bed and I stand up with her.

"It's 1pm. You didn't show up at lunch so I came to check up on you." She heads to the bathroom and I follow her.

She closes the bathroom's door but not before I notice a bloody hand towel and bandages on the counter.

The fuck?

I push the door open and look around. There's blood in the sink and Valeri is there staring at it.

"What the fuck did you do?"

AN: -word count- 1500

I'm back!!!

What do you think? Will Valeri open up to Zach? What will be his reaction?

If you're struggling with your mental health please try to reach out for help<3

Bye!!

14

"**W**hat the fuck did you do?"

I stare at the blood in the sink. What did I do?

"I got a nosebleed." I mutter trying to hide the truth. I can't look Zach in the eyes because I know he will see that I'm lying.

"You don't need a bandage when you nosebleed, Valeri." He says slowly as he looks at me.

I just stare at the sink ignoring his wondering eyes. Mine fill with tears so I look away. Away from him. Away from blood.

Wait I didn't lock the door? How could I forget? I told myself I will clean everything up when I wake up because I was tired but it looks like I forgot to do it.

I quickly wipe my tears not wanting him to notice.

"Valeri." Zach whispers.

"It's not what you think it is." I whisper.

"Then what happened?"

"I've already told you I had a nosebleed." I shrug with my shoulders and start cleaning the dried blood.

"Why did you need a bandage?" He's behind me looking at my face through the mirror.

"I was just searching for something to stop it and I found a bandage but I knew it won't help so I just left it here on the counter." I say the first thing that comes into my mind.

Zach looks unsure but his face softens. "Oh. Okay." He says still searching my face.

I want to tell him so bad.

He doesn't believe me, does he?

ZACHARY

The first thing that comes in my mind is self harm. Does Valeri still do it?

She told me it was just a nosebleed and it kind of makes sense now. I was overreacting. It was nothing.

But she still didn't look in my eyes. Was she lying?

Nah I'm definitely overreacting even though I was worried sick last night because of the way she rushed out of my room.

"Oh. Okay." I say. "Do I help you clean up?" I add after a few moments.

"No that's okay."

"Alright. Come downstairs after you finish." I step closer to her and hug her.

She freezes but then returns the hug.

Then I leave her room.

VALERI

I have no idea how I got away with it but I feel sort of relieved even though a part of me wanted to tell Zach everything.

He left me alone in the bathroom as he went back downstairs.

I know he didn't truly believe me. He looked so confused and worried. What was he thinking? About self harm?

Yup he definitely thought that I hurt myself.

I mean it's true but still.

I lock my bathroom door and hop up on the counter. First I take off the bandage on my wrist. I see the cuts stopped bleeding and are starting to heal. I take some gauze and put it on. Then I take off the bandages on my thighs and do the same.

As I'm done I dress up again and get out to my bedroom.

Dizziness overcomes me and I have to lean on a wall to keep myself standing.

Fuck I didn't eat anything and lost too much blood this morning.

I put on a sweater and head downstairs.

They all look up when I enter the kitchen.

"Valeri. We missed you." Lach stands up and hugs me. Pain shoots through my wrists as I squeeze him back.

"You excited for another party tonight?" Madelin smiles at me.

A party? Another one? Fuck fuck fuck.

"Who will be there?" I ask as I sit down on a chair.

"The same as the last time. Except for Cade and those assholes. They left a couple of hours ago."

Good.

I take some food and start eating. The conversation goes on but I don't follow because I'm overwhelmed with voices in my head that keep telling me I should stop.

"I'm going swimming. It's too hot in here." Lach says and leaves.

Mers and Ayna nod in agreement and go after him. And then the others too.

So I'm alone now. No one is here.

Cade isn't here. It's okay.

I look around the kitchen and stare at the cabinet from which one I stole the painkillers. There must be more.

I get up and go closer.

I hear others having fun in the pool so I open the cabinet and look.

There isn't much. Just some painkillers. But I don't need them right now. I still have some upstairs in my room. Plus others will definitely notice they're gone so I put it back.

I pour myself some water instead and go outside on the yard to join my friends.

Why is it so hot here?

I run up to my room and put on some basketball shorts because I can't stand it anymore. I wish I could put off my hoodie too but I know I can't. No one can find out.

I make sure the gauze and scars can't be seen and go back outside. I sit down on a deckchair and watch Mers trying to sneak behind Lach.

I close my eyes for a bit but then someone interrupts me.

"Aren't you hot?" Zach asks as he sits on a deckchair next to mine.

Is he trying to get a reaction out of me? Well, he won't get one.

"Hotter then you obviously." I mutter.

He narrows his eyes and I wink at him. He's definitely blushing now and I laugh to myself in my head.

"Why aren't you swimming?"

"Why aren't you?" I tease him.

He's quiet for some time looking at me. "Because I know Lach would try to drown me." He laughs and gives Lach death stare.

I chuckle.

"So. How have you been?" Zach asks.

Really bad. I feel like shit.

"Good." I shrug with my shoulders. "Really good. Why are you asking?"

"Just wanted to know."

We are quiet for some time.

"Wanna go swimming?" Zach breaks the silence.

Shit.

"Nah, I'm good. You should though."

He searches my face. "Nah I'll stay here with you."

Perfect.

I close my eyes ignoring him.

"Sooo..." he starts.

"Let me sleep." I cut him off.

"Yes ma'am." He shuts up.

But I can't sleep without pills. Every time I want to, I feel their touch between my legs, their fingernails cutting my skin trying to hold me down and the pain after they hit me.

~~~

The night has fallen and I can hear music downstairs. I'm in the same clothes I was the whole day.

Even though I know Cade isn't here anymore, I still don't feel comfortable showing much skin.

I've taken two pills to calm down my nerves. The problem with them is that when I want to fall asleep I have to take lots of them otherwise it doesn't work. That means I run out of them really quick.

I have just a few left. Enough for later tonight but I have no idea what I'll do tomorrow.

I unlock the door and go downstairs. The music is louder here.

I walk through the kitchen and finally spot my friends on the couch.

"Hey." I say and drop down next to my brother with a sigh.

"Valeri, hey, where were you?" Alex asks.

"Upstairs."

He nods and continues with a conversation with the boys. I have no idea where Madelin, Mers and Ayna are though.

"Girls are at the pool." Alex says like he read my mind.

"Alright." I get up. "See ya." I walk through the kitchen first and pour myself vodka or something. It burns my throat as I swallow it.

I walk outside to the pool where others should be. It looks like they're having so much fun. They're all in the water. Madelin is talking to someone and Mers and Ayna are in the corner making out.

I knew it.

I walk to the couches and sit down.

There's a group of guys and girls here. They look pretty fucked. High.

After some time they all stand up and go inside. Except for one guy.

I watch him as he takes some pills from his pocket. I watch him swallow one of them and see him calm down immediately.

This is my chance.

Should I? Shouldn't I?

I stand up.

Should I?

I get a bit closer and sit down next to him trying to not make it obvious yet.

Should I trust him? The last time I did, it didn't end well.

But my gut is telling me he isn't dangerous.

He pulls small bag of white powder from his bag now. He shakes it down on the table and does a line.

Is this a bad idea? Fuck it.

"Hey." I say.

AN: -word count- 1455

A cliffhanger again!! Sorry not sorry.

I'm listening to The Weeknd rn. They're the best. Who's your favourite artist?

So, what do you think about the story? Where is this going? I honestly don't know either. I have some ideas but we'll see.

You can give ideas too!!! Please comment.

If you're struggling with your mental health please try to reach out for help<3

Don't forget to vote.

I love u! Bye

15

- -

He turns to me. His arm is covered in tatoos that run up from his fingers to his neck. His hair is bleached.

"You want some?" He nudges at the powder.

"I- umm... no thanks." I think for a bit. "Do you have anything that would help me fall asleep?" I say quietly.

He's quiet.

"Yeah sure. But it will cost you." He warns.

"How much?" I ask.

"It depends on how much you need, of course." He explains.

"Umm okay. Uhh-" I have no idea how this shit works.

"Here." He cuts me off and pulls some from his bag and shows me. "Is this enough or do you need more?"

"It's enough, I guess." I nod.

"Alright. But we shouldn't do this here." He looks around.

What should I do? Do I trust him?

"Upstairs, second door on the left." I say and walk away in the house. Alex can't see me with him. No one can.

I look over my shoulder and see the guy walk a few metres behind me. I go up the stairs into my room.

A few seconds later the door closes behind me and I turn around.

"Your first time?" He asks curiously.

I take a deep breath. "First time buying. I've done it before though."

He nods and puts a bag on my bed. He takes out the pills he showed me a few minutes ago.

"What are these?" I ask.

"Sleeping pills."

I inhale. Okay. I can do it.

"Okay."

I open my bag in the wardrobe and pull some money from my wallet. Our so called 'dad' that I haven't seen in weeks left me and Alex some. I have savings from months ago too so it isn't a problem.

I turn back to the guy. He's watching me.

"Here." I put cash in his hand. "Is this enough?"

He looks down. "Yeah."

He gives me sleeping pills. There is twenty or thirty of them. "Take one or two the most, okay?"

I slowly nod. I did it. There's no going back now.

"If you ever need someone to talk to, I'm here to listen." He says quietly.

"Okay. Thanks." I nod again and put the pills in my drawer.

"Where can I find you if I need more?"

He looks down at me. "Where's your phone?"

I take it out of my pocket and give it to him.

He starts putting his number in but stops. "You don't have a burner phone, do you?"

I think about it. My mother had one. Fuck. I go to my bag and search a side pocket.

I pull it out. Here it is. My mother's burner phone.

I took it right before the police arrived. I don't know why, I just didn't want them to know about it.

I open it and give it to the guy.

He takes it still curiously looking at me but then saves his number on it.

I shove it back from where I found it.

"Ryan." He introduces himself.

"And you must be Alex's sister Valeri, right?"

ZACHARY

I've just used the bathroom in my room and as I'm done I get out on the hallway. I look around to make sure no one is hooking up in any of our rooms. It's disgusting.

I turn to the stairs but something catches my eyes. Someone.

And that someone just stepped out of Valeri's room. He's still turned to the door so I can't know who it is. But I can hear Valeri talking.

Is she safe?

When I decide I should get closer and check if she's okay, the guy turns around.

The fuck was she doing with Ryan? I thought she was outside with Madelin and others.

I know who Ryan is because he goes to our school. I've never disliked him but I know what he does. That's why I don't like him being in Valeri's presence. He's a good guy and I know he wouldn't do anything to harm her but still. She had problems with an addiction-maybe she still does from what I saw this morning- and I know she wouldn't be able to stop without help, if she tries anything else.

Fuck. She has been so distant this past week it makes me worry. I don't know what to say about what happened in the morning. The way she said It isn't what you think it is made me worry the worst. She thought that I thought she was self harming. That tells me something. Was she lying? And she always wears long sleeves and she haven't swum yet since we came here. Except for the first day when Lach threw her in the pool. But she had clothes on.

I go back in my room and hear Ryan walk down the stairs. I need to talk to Valeri. Make sure she's doing okay.

I step back on the hall right when she does the same. She's putting on a hoodie.

Did they-

Valeri looks at me but quickly walks past. It looks like she forgot to roll her sleeves back down.

She knows I saw him but I does she know I also saw her fresh cuts.

VALERI

Shit. Shit. Shit.

I know Zach saw us. Saw him. Fuck.

I quickly walk past him without saying anything and run down the stairs. I hear him behind me. I go in the kitchen and take a drink and then go outside. I need to get out of here. I run down to the beach.

It's obvious that Zach knows Ryan. The look on his face told me everything.

I'm walking through the sand with a bottle in my hand.

I can't hear if Zach followed me because of the wind but I don't care. I don't stop until I come to the water.

It's full moon tonight so I can easily see around me. I see him.

He followed me.

I really don't want to talk to him. I don't even want to look at him. Did he realise what we were doing?

I take a sip. And a few more. This can't be happening.

Zach reaches me.

"Valeri stop." He's right infront of me.

"What do you want?" I drink some more.

"To check if you're okay."

"Why wouldn't I be?" I lie.

The alcohol kicked in by now.

"How much did you have?"

Is he talking about pills? Does he know?

"Huh?" I stutter.

"For fuck's sake, Valeri." He takes the bottle from my hand.

I try to pull it back but he won't let me so I give up. We're both quiet looking at each other.

"Why did you lie, gorgeous?" He asks. His face is only a few inches from mine.

The fuck is he talking about?

"What?" I'm so confused and alcohol isn't helping.

"You know what I mean." He takes my hand.

I try to pull away again but he won't let me. He isn't harsh like they were though. His touch is soft and gentle.

Zach starts pulling up my sleeve but I realise what he's doing.

"No." I say.

He immediately stops. "I know about them. I know you lied this morning. I saw them when you were coming out of your room. With Ryan." He whispers.

That's when I realise my mistake. How could I forget?

I start shaking my head. This isn't supposed to be happening. No. He shouldn't know. No one should. Tears make my vision blurry and I can't stop them from falling down my cheeks.

Zach's hand is there now. He wipes them away with his fingers. "It's okay."

He pulls me close and wraps his arms around me. I bury my face in his neck and silently sob.

He gives me a kiss on the top of my head. "It's okay, gorgeous." He whispers.

I don't know if I'll ever be able to look at him. What if he sees me differently now?

I close my eyes and take a deep breath.

Okay he knows about that. But that doesn't mean he knows about other things.

I exhale.

I think I drank too much. Dizziness stops me from thinking straight.

"Zach?"

"Yeah?"

"I think I had too much. I don't feel very well." I mumble.

"That's okay, let's go back." He puts his arm over my shoulder and we head back to the house.

"Please don't tell Alex." I beg him.

He sighs. "I won't."

We make it back and go up the stairs. Everything is spinning and I miss a step.

Zach is there to catch me and picks me up like last time. I don't know in whose room we are now but we are suddenly in the bathroom.

I throw up in a toilet as soon as Zach puts me down.

And it happens again. I feel my heart start racing and I try to breathe but it feels like there isn't enough oxygen.

I feel someone hold my hair up and stroke my back. It must be Zach.

I'm sweating like hell now and I have no idea what's happening.

"You're burning up." He nudges at my hoodie. "Can I take it off?"

I don't say anything.

"Valeri. Look at me."

I do.

There's a question in his eyes and I slowly nod.

I feel him pull my hoodie over my head. I know he'll see my scars.

The colder air hits my arms as I'm kneeling there with my tee-shirt on.

But he doesn't stop to look at them. He just gives me a paper towel to wipe my mouth with it.

I do it and sit down on cold tiles with my back to the wall as I try to breathe in.

I hear a toilet flush and then someone sits down beside me and pulls me into him.

I close my eyes.

We stay in each other's arms until someone opens bathroom door.

AN: -word count- 1656

A cliffhanger AGAIN!

I don't know if everything is rushed. I mean we are only on 15th chapter and Zach already knows Valeri harms herself.

There might not be another chapter for a few days because I'm starting school again

ANYWAY DOES ANYONE HAVE A VALENTINE? I don't :(

If you're struggling with your mental health please try to reach out for help.

I ♡ u! Byee

16

We stay in each other's arms until someone opens bathroom door.

Zach quickly stands up and drops a hoodie over my arms.

My brother.

"Zach? Valeri, what are you doing here?" Alex kneels infront of me and makes sure I'm okay. "What happened?"

"I just don't feel good. I drank too much." I explain.

He puts arms around me and leans his chin on my head. "I couldn't find you anywhere. I was worried sick." Alex caresses my hair.

"I'm better now." I mutter.

He stands up beside Zach and I pull the sweatshirt over my head. I make sure Alex can't see what I do to myself. He won't want me if he finds out.

I stand up on shaky legs and black dots take my vision away again. I can't see anything for a few seconds but I can feel someone holding me up. I feel their touch on my waist and my arm, how careful they are with my body and scars.

I blink and black dots swim away and leave me with a light of Zach's bathroom. He and Alex are standing infront of me with worry written all over their faces.

"Are you okay, gorgeous?" Zach asks me.

Am I?

I nod.

He leads me out of the bathroom with Alex following after us. Zach carefully helps me in his bed and covers me with a blanket.

"You can sleep here." He reassuringly smiles at me.

My brother kisses my forehead and looks at me.

"You don't have to. I'll be okay." I weakly smile.

"Okay. Love you, sis." He whispers and leaves the room.

It's just me and Zach now and there's no way I can look at him.

He saw them. He doesn't want you here. He's disgusted by you.

I close my eyes.

I feel Zachary sit down on the other side of his bed.

"I understand if you don't want to be my friend anymore." My voice is shaking. In my head I beg him to not look at me differently.

"What?" I can hear shock in his voice. He gets closer to me but I keep my eyes closed.

After I don't say anything he hugs me.

He hugs me?

Zach's arms are embracing my shoulders and his chin is rested on my head as he slowly kisses my hair.

I don't understand.

"What do you not understand?" He whispers.

I said that out loud?

"Hmm?" He kisses my head again. "I care about you. So much."

"You do? You don't care about... " I trail off. I don't want to say it.

"No, I don't. I really really like being around you. The fact that you're having a hard time and you harm yourself won't change that, okay?" He takes my hand and interlocks our fingers.

I stare at our locked hands.

He doesn't care about that?

"What about Alex? I- I can't tell him. Never. What if he sees me differently and he won't care about me anymore?" I look up at Zach and he looks stunned.

"You don't seriously think that, do you?"

I shrug with my shoulders.

"Your brother loves you and nothing could ever change that. Believe me when I tell you that he would willingly die if that meant making you happy."

"Really?" I stare at his bright green eyes. Our faces are only inches apart and I can feel his breath on my cheek.

"Really. He would do anything for you." Zach is now holding my jaw in his hand. I see his eyes look down at my lips and back up.

I think I want to kiss him.

I touch his cheek with one hand and trail my fingers through his dark hair with the other one.

Zach leans in until our lips almost touch. "And I'd do anything for you, too, gorgeous." He whispers and covers my lips with his.

He kisses me slowly with passion and I freeze for a second but then kiss him back.

His lips are soft and warm and I can feel butterflies in my stomach.

We both pull back and stare in each other's eyes and then I remember.

"Did you forget I threw up not even thirty minutes ago?"

He smiles at me and puts his forehead on mine. "Yup."

I shove him with my elbow and cover my face with my palms. Zach pulls them away and leans in for another kiss but I get up.

"I'll be right back. I'll just get my things, okay?" I say and kiss his cheek because I don't want him to taste my vomit again. Okay that sounded weird.

I step in the hallway. I can still hear music and other people downstairs.

What has just happened? Zach kissed me? Am I dreaming? Oh my- I can't believe this. It felt too right.

I enter my room, shower and change in Zach's hoodie. Before I go back I brush my teeth and look at myself in the mirror.

I smile.

I go back in my bedroom and look around.

"Be quiet, you whore."

I blink and flashbacks end. I take a deep breath and open a drawer of my bedside table. I take two pills that Ryan gave me and put them in my pocket for later because I can't sleep without them.

I make my way back on the hallway and knock before I open Zach's bedroom door. It looks like he has just gotten out of the shower because his hair aren't completely dry yet and he's wearing different clothes.

"Hey, gorgeous." Zach says with a smile and approaches me.

"Hi." I can't say anything else because I'm too busy blushing.

He puts a strand of hair behind my ear and leans in. My breath hitches. "Did you brush your teeth, gorgeous?" He asks with a grin on his face.

Just kiss me already.

I have enough of his games so I pull him closer by his necklace.

His soft lips land on mine and I kiss him back. He opens mine as his tongue makes his way in.

What does this man do to me-

I moan a little as I feel his tongue.

I want to slap that smirk off his face now.

I feel my back hit the door behind me as Zach deepens the kiss. He starts kissing my jaw and neck but I can feel him holding back as if he's waiting for my consent.

"I can't. I'm sorry, Zach." I whisper. He stops immediately and looks me in my eyes. Gosh I feel horrible for stopping him.

"That's okay, Valeri. As much as I want to I think it's too soon." Zach says.

"I agree."

The thing is that it isn't a problem that it's too soon but I just can't. Not with still feeling their hands on my body.

I kiss Zach again to convince myself this is real and just because I like kissing him, obviously.

He picks me up and I wrap my legs around his waist and my arms around his neck. He gently puts his palms on my lower back so I don't fall.

Zach lies down on his bed with me still on top of him. I lean my head on his chest and breathe. He feels like home. He really does.

"Are you tired?" He whispers and I nod.

He then lands kisses all over my face. My cheeks, forehead, my nose and lastly on my lips.

I laugh and bury my head in the crook of his neck. I feel him playing with my long hair.

I want to stay like this forever.

He turns the light off and we're lying in a complete darkness now.

I'm really tired but I can't sleep if I have nightmares so I wait for some time and then carefully reach in my pocket and take out two sleeping pills. I swallow them without water and exhale.

Will I ever stop doing this? Will I ever stop cutting myself? Will I ever stop starving? Will I ever be happy?

I am happy when I'm with my friends and especially Zachary but I can't keep off my mind what Cade and his friend, who I don't even know the name of, did to me.

I sigh and close my eyes. I wait until the pills kick in and darkness consumes me.

ZACHARY

I'm lying on my back and my girl is lying on top of me. I feel her move a little but then she calms down and her breathing slows.

Valeri is breathtaking. Literally every inch of her is perfect.

And we kissed today. We kissed! She likes me back!

I kiss the top of her head again and make myself comfortable.

So many things happened today but we'll talk about everything in the morning.

And of course I have to ask her if she wants me to be her boyfriend. I'm pretty nervous about that one.

I don't know if she even wants to be in a relationship right now. She's dealing with some shit but I really hope she does.

I try to inhale and exhale at the same time as Valeri until I fall asleep.

AN: -word count- 1533

Heyy my loves❤

What do you think about the story? About Valeri and Zach?

I opened Wattpad and I was greeted with more than 1k reads on this story. Oh my god I'm so so so so so happy about it! I still remember when I posted the first chapter and four people read it. I was so excited about it!

Okay so this is chapter 16. I don't know how long should I do this story but I'm thinking about 25-30 chapters. Please comment if you think that would be too short or too long. I have some ideas but I don't think I can make more than 30 with them.

I don't know why I'm telling you this but my parents are arguing right now so writing this chapter helped me forget it :/

If you're struggling with your mental health please try to reach out for help!

I love u all<3

17

I wake up in someone's arms. Zach is lying behind me with my back to his front, his arm is around my waist and I can feel his warm breath on my neck.

Everything that happened yesterday comes back and I smile.

I slowly turn around trying to not wake Zach up but it's too late. He's already staring at me with those beautiful green eyes.

Before I can say anything, he catches my mouth with his and pulls me into a warm kiss.

He gently pushes me on my back and he's now on top of me. He buries his head in my neck like I did yesterday and I stroke his messy hair.

"Hi." He mumbles with that sleepy morning voice.

"Hey." I whisper in his hair.

We stay like that for some time.

"I have to go to the bathroom." I say quietly because I don't know if he's asleep again.

He protests but then lets me out. I stand up and darkness comes back. Zach puts his arms around me and after a few seconds I can normally see again. I sit down on the bed with Zach hugging me from behind.

"You okay?"

"Yeah. It's just low iron and bad blood flow." I tell him.

"Oh. Are you taking meds?" He asks.

Which ones?

I'm kidding.

I shake with my head.

"Tell me or Alex if you need them and we will drive you to a doctor, okay?"

"Yeah." I get up again and go in the bathroom.

I do my business, wash my face and then take a deep breath as I stare at myself in the mirror. I lift up my shirt and pull down my pants so I can see my thighs. Will the bruises ever fade? Will my scars? I close my eyes when their voice comes back.

But another thought quiets those. There's a chance I'm pregnant, isn't there?

My periods are irregular because of my mental health and all the things I'm dealing with, so I can't just wait a week to see if I'm late. It could take months. I don't think I'm pregnant, though.

Zach is still lying on his bed watching me when I come back.

I smile trying to cover up how I'm feeling. Will I ruin him with my problems? Will he leave me if I tell him?

I notice he noticed my mood shifted so I quickly get back in bed and he puts a blanket over me.

Fuck. I really need it.

"You okay?"

I nod with my head on his chest so he can't see my face. I just stare at the door. I need it so bad.

I feel him kiss my head.

I lift my head up and kiss him on the lips when we get interrupted. Someone opens the door.

"Why do I always catch you two together in bed?" Lach yells as he makes sure everybody in this house hears.

Zach looks at me apologeticly and throws Lach out of the room.

Then I go in my room and lock myself in the bathroom. I take the blade and put it on my left wrist. I press it down on my bruised skin and pull it across. I do it again and then do it on my thighs over the ones that started fading. It's just a few cuts.

I stand up and my legs are shaking as pain shoots through my arm. The fuck did I do now?

I just stand there, staring at my cuts, at what I did. I wait for the blood to stop and then I clean everything up.

Zach is waiting for me in the hallway. I feel so bad. There's finally something good in my life but I still can't help it.

Everyone is already downstairs. From their bored face expressions, it looks like they were waiting for us for quite a long time.

Alex and Lach hug me and ask if I'm okay.

Mers of course has to make inappropriate comments about me and Zach and about what we were 'doing' the whole night.

We go on the beach like every other day. I don't swim and Zach is waiting here with me.

"Let's go for a walk." He takes my hand and pulls me up.

We go away from the others but we are still walking by the sea. Zach is holding my hand but everything feels so far away.

We stop.

"So I wanted to ask you something." He looks nervous.

"Go on." I encourage him.

He's quiet for some time but then finally asks. "Can I be your boyfriend?" His cheeks turn red.

He's asking me to be with him? In a relationship?

I almost nod but then I remember. Zach looks confused.

"Did I do something wrong?" He asks searching my face.

I shake with my head and hug him. "It's just that... I'm dealing with some things and maybe I will be really distant some days. I just get those episodes... " I trail off as I'm playing with my fingers.

Zach lifts my head up and pecks my nose. "I'll help you, okay? If you need to talk, I'll be here."

"Yeah I know, but there are some days when I completely distance myself from everybody and I want to be alone. I mean it's just too hard for me and I don't want to bother anyone else."

"You could never bother me with your problems, gorgeous. I'll help you go through every day and I'll give you space when you need it."

He would?

I consider everything and then I nod. "Yes."

"Yes, what?"

I kiss him.

He pulls me closer by my waist and I trail my fingers through his hair. We continue this for quite a long time.

The day comes and goes and it's already evening now. We're having a bonfire on the beach.

It's dark and I can hear the sound of the waves and wind. We're all sitting down on the sand and Zach is slowly kissing my neck. He's sitting behind me and I'm leaning on him with my back.

He's holding my left hand and I play with his fingers.

"Are you nervous? You seem like you are." He asks quietly. I shake with my head but I don't stop.

Zach touches my left wrist and I flinch back because of the pain. He stills and hugs me tighter.

"You clean them, right?" He whispers so no one can hears it except for me.

"Yeah." I nod and he puts his arms around my shoulders and leans his chin on my head. "Good. I'm here if you ever need help with it."

I know he doesn't mean only the cuts but other things too.

Everyone have been watching us for the whole day and they don't stop. I don't know why this is a big deal.

ZACHARY

Everybody is curiously looking at us. It's probably because I've never shown interest in anyone. I've had a few girlfriends, of course, but it was nothing serious and others knew it.

My heart has always belonged to one person and I am with that special person right now. I'm so happy.

I know I should tell her the truth but I don't know if she would still want me after it. I think I would just drag her back into her past. And believe me, her past was not great. It's better to ask for forgiveness. I mean I know I'll tell her one day but that day isn't today. I also know I'm selfish. I can't risk losing her.

She's sitting between my legs as I'm hugging her from behind. I'm putting soft kisses on her neck. However, I can't unnotice how she's playing with my fingers.

"Are you nervous? You seem like you are." I say in her ear but she shakes with her head.

I take her hand but she flinches and quickly moves it away. The fuck? Did she relapse? When? Or are these still the old ones?

I just hope she takes care of them carefully, so they don't get infected. "You clean them, right? I whisper.

"Yeah." She nods.

"Good. I'm here if you ever need help with it." I don't mean it only about her harming herself but about everything she's going through. I hope one day she will tell me what's going on in her head.

I hope one day she will trust me enough to open up to me.

AN: -word count- 1419

I was dealing with some things this week, so I wasn't able to write, but here it is.

Anyway, how are you? How was your day?

Do you have any ideas for next chapters? If so, feel free to comment.

Don't forget to vote!

I love u, byee!!

18

Today is the day we are going home. I'm happy about it because I won't have to make excuses why I didn't swim and I just want to get away from this place as soon as possible. I want to leave the bad memories behind.

It has been a few days since Zach asked me to be his girlfriend and I really really really like him. He's probably the best person I've ever met and he makes me feel special. Though I have him now, I'm still not feeling alright. I can't forget their touch and voice. I secretly take sleeping pills before I go to sleep or take a nap, otherwise I wouldn't be able to. And I sometimes take painkillers through the day to prevent panic attacks even though they don't always help.

Yup, I only have half of the pills Ryan gave me. I have no idea how am I already running out because I honestly don't remember taking that much.

I'm packing my stuff right now. There's not much, so it doesn't take long. I've been sleeping in Zach's bed and I just come into my room to shower and change and you know what.

I want to stop but I can't. I want to stop for Zach. He's treating me like a goddess but I can't prevent myself from doing it. Am I selfish? Am I an attention seeker? Am I even worth anything?

As I'm done I make sure I don't forget the pills and other things I need. And then I go out of my room. Zach joins me and takes my bag.

"I can do it myself."

"I know, but I want to do it for you." Yeah, he's been a gentleman the whole week.

I look at my room for the last time and hope I'll never have to come here again.

I sigh and go after him. I don't feel well. I feel like gravity is too strong today.

We make it to the car and Zach loads the luggage in.

Madelin approaches me from behind and hugs me. "Heyy! You want to go with us?"

I look at Zach and he reassuringly smiles at me.

"Sure," I'm actually really excited to drive with girls since I spent most of the time with Zach.

I hug my boy and my brother and then we go in. Mers is driving and I'm in the back with Madelin.

"Girl, we almost didn't see you for the past week." Ayna says from the passenger seat.

"She was too busy doing you know what with Zach." Madelin laughs.

This reminds me of Cade and his friend. I still don't know what his name is.

"Ughh I'm too gay for that." Mers looks at me with fake disgust.

I put on a smile but my hands are shaking. It looks like they're waiting for me to say something. "Yeah we didn't do that. We aren't like you and Ayna who can't help themselves and do it in public." I roll my eyes and laugh.

Mers smirks and Ayna blushes.

"What were you doing if not that?" Madelin asks me and I shrug with my shoulders.

I look out the window and ignore the conversation they're having. I even drift off for a bit but not much.

"Can't blame you. You have to live with Cade." His name brings me back into present but I keep my eyes closed.

"Yeah and those motherfuckers are there 24/7. I literally can't even rest because I have to look at their stupid faces and listen to their disgusting voices."

"For real. I have no idea how could Zach hang out with them a few years ago. I actually don't even know why they stopped, I just noticed that they despise each other now."

ZACHARY

I think I'm falling in love with Valeri again. She's so precious and caring. I fell in love with her years ago and I think I haven't stopped ever since. We lost so much time with those three years we were apart. My family adopted me when I was a baby and they loved me as if I was truly theirs. And then when I was fifteen we moved away. My parents work around the world so they aren't at home much. I sometimes see them every few months so I just stay at Alex's house. The whole time I was away I was worrying about Valeri. I wasn't even sure she was alive until one day when Alex told me he has a twin sister named Valeri. He told me from where she is and what happened and I immediately knew.

Though Valeri saw me only as her best friend, I was in love with her. Of course I never told her that plus we were so young. She was fourteen and I was fifteen but we were born the same year, my birthday is just half a year before hers. She actually has it in a bit more then two weeks. Alex too, obviously.

I wish she was here with me right now but she's driving with girls. I hope she's having fun.

"So, what's with you and Valeri?" Kian asks.

I smile when he mentions my girl. Alex looks at me from the driver's seat. I don't know what's his opinion on me dating his sister but I hope he doesn't mind it.

"Come on, dude, is she your girlfriend?" Kian continues and Alex looks curiously looks at me. He's wondering too.

"Yeah, she is." I smile.

"You're so in love, man."

"Yeah." I mutter under my breath but I know Alex heard me because I'm sitting on the passenger's seat.

My best friend looks at me again and I understand what he's trying to say.

We'll talk about it later.

I nod.

~~~

"If you break her heart, Zach, I'll fucking kill you."

We're currently in his room arguing. Valeri took a nap in her room after long ride but she can probably hear us.

"I won't. I promise."

"Okay." Alex sighs and sits down next to me. "I'm just ... After you told me about her past I just can't help but worry. She deserves so much more. She deserves you. But ... you're my best friend and it's just so so weird."

"I know." I want to tell him that Valeri isn't doing well, but I know it's not my thing to tell.

VALERI

I wake up after a few hours and everything hurts me. Fuck, I must take a pregnancy test. However, I can't ask Zach or Alex to get me one and I don't drive.

I should text Madelin. She's my closest girl friend.

Madelin

Me: hey, could you drive me to the store?

I wait for a few minutes and then she finally replies.

Madelin: ofc!! When? x

Me: could you pick me up now?

Madelin: sure. I'll be there in ten.

I put the phone away and go change. After that, I go to Alex's room. I knock and open the door. Both my brother and Zach are lying on the bed.

Zach gets up and gives me a kiss. Did he forget my brother is in the same room?

He pulls back and I smile at him. He's so pretty.

I turn to my brother who is trying to look away. "Hey. Can I go out with Madelin? She's picking me up now."

"You aren't tired anymore?" Alex gets up.

"I slept for a few hours."

"Alright. I'll pick you up later, okay? Call me. And don't get drunk like you did the last time."

I nod.

We go downstairs to the kitchen as we wait for Madelin.

We hear a car a few minutes later and I hug Alex and kiss Zach goodbye. Then I go outside and I'm greeted with Madelin.

I open the car's door. "Hiii." She hugs me and I squeeze her back. "How are you?"

"I'm good, you?"

"Like always. So. Where are we going?"

"To the store. The closest one. And then we can hang out for a bit more, I you'd like." I say.

"Of course." She starts the car and we pull out of the driveway.

We talk about movies through the whole ride until we get to the store.

We enter it. "So, what do you need?" She asks looking at food.

I can tell her. She will just think I had sex with Zach and everything will be okay. But the truth is, there's a chance I'm pregnant with her cousin.

I exhale. "A pregnancy test."

Madelin turns her head to look at me. "What?"

I just stand there.

"You said you and Zach didn't ... ohh, you lied, didn't you?" She smiles.

"Yeah." I lie.

"Follow me." She takes my hand. "You think you're pregnant? Holy fuck." We walk past perfumes.

"I don't know. I just want to make sure." I say.

We finally see them and I take two different ones. Then she takes me to the isle with alcohol.

Yup. Good combination.

Madelin takes a bottle of vodka and we head to the cash-register. We put the things to the lady at the counter and she gives us a look.

Yup. I don't know what to say, but I can see Madelin is trying not to laugh.

We pay and go out.

"We can go to mine if you'd like." She offers.

What if Cade is there? I'll just have to ignore him.

"Okay."

We drive away and go past my house. There's a car a few doors down and someone gets out of it and goes to unlock the door.

Ryan.

AN: -word count- 1609

What do you think? Is she pregnant? Do you want her to be?

I put some of Zachary's past in this chapter.

I have a few ideas for the next chapters and I think they're really good, so I hope you'll like what's coming.

Also, should I do a 'chapter' about characters (their names, age, what they're like)?? Please comment.

Don't forget to vote:)

Have a nice day<3

19

R yan.

We make a quick eye contact before we speed off. We drive for around another ten minutes until we pull infront of a big house.

On the way to her bedroom I keep looking around to make sure Cade isn't here. I think he wouldn't do anything if Madelin is with me the whole time.

She opens her door and I'm greeted with a huge room. It has really big windows and bed but it looks comfy.

"Make yourself feel like home." She jumps on her bed with a bag from the store. "So. Aren't you going to take the test?"

I take the bag and take both of them out. "You're not pregnant, okay? He used protection, didn't he?" She asked.

"Yeah, he did." They didn't.

"Go on, then." I do as she says and go into the bathroom. There's a bath and a shower.

I open the package and follow instructions. It's written that I have to wait fifteen minutes.

I leave it on a counter and go back in the room.

I can't be pregnant. I'm an addict and I was taking pills and harming myself for the last two weeks.

"You okay?" Madelin asks with alcohol in her hand.

"Yeah. I have to wait for some time." I sit down next to her.

She hugs me and we stay like that for some time. "You should go check."

I take a deep breath and nod. I get off the bed and enter the bathroom again. There it is.

It's negative.

I'm not pregnant.

I let out a sigh of relief and throw the test in the trash. Then I go back in the bedroom. Madelin is lying on her back drinking out of the bottle.

"Easy there." I take it away and take a sip myself.

"You aren't pregnant?" She asks and throws her arms around me. She's clearly drunk. I tuck her in the bed as she falls asleep. She must've been really tired and the alcohol helped.

I lie down beside her and stare at the ceiling. I take three painkillers out of my pocket and swallow them with vodka. Fuck I've just run out of them. I'll have to ask Ryan for more but not now. Maybe tomorrow.

I almost drift off until a knock interrupts me. Fuck fuck fuck. Who the fuck is that?

I can't think straight because of everything I took and I have no time to hide.

The door opens revealing a guy.

No no no. Just not him.

He looks shocked when he sees me but a smile pushes his surprised expression away. "Valeri. What are you doing here?" Cade asks.

I try to reach for my phone but he stops my hand. The pain shoots through my arm as he squeezes my wrist. My cuts.

"Please don't. I'm begging you." I try to shake Madelin awake but she must be passed out completely.

I look back at Cade, at his blue eyes and blond hair. He's still holding me and pushes me down on the bed so he's now on top. "You'll listen to me now, you hear me?" When I don't answer he hits me. "You hear me?"

I quickly nod and don't stop. "Good. Now, you'll break up with your boyfriend. You'll break his heart, okay? Do you understand?!" He hisses as I don't answer him. I shake with my head. I can't do this to Zachary.

He starts unbuckling his pants. "This is your last chance to say yes. To say that you'll do as I told you to, otherwise you know what is going to happen."

I'm sorry Zach, my love, but I can't go through this again...

It takes me a few seconds but I finally spit it out. "Yes, I'll do as you said."

"What are you going to do?"

"I'm going to break up with him."

"If I find out you're lying, I'll tell every single one of your friends that you're buying from Ryan and that we had sex because you were so desperate for it. And me and Marc will find you and do it again and again until you do listen to us, you understand? Maybe we'll even invite someone else with us." He smirks down at me. I blink the tears away and I hear him put on his belt again and I sigh out. "You're a slut. Don't forget that." He kisses my neck hard and I know he's going to leave a hickey.

Then he gets off me and leaves the room with a slam of the door.

A loud sob leaves my mouth and I try to be silent so I don't wake Madelin up. I look at her. She looks so peaceful. If she knew what has just happened...

"Fuck." I whisper. I get up on my shaking legs and go in Madelin's bathroom. I search all of the cabinets until I find some pills. I don't even check what they are for before I swallow them.

My breathing slows down and I look in my reflection. A broken girl stares back at me. A slut. There's a black bruise forming on her left cheek and one on her left wrist. The one covered in cuts she did herself. A red hickey is decorating her neck. A hickey she didn't want.

And then I realise. That girl is me. Me. That broken used body is mine. That face is mine. That mind is mine.

I wash my face and search the drawers. I'm sure Madelin won't wake up before morning and I know she wouldn't mind me borrowing her makeup. I cover my cheek and then my neck. But I can't cover up my wrists because the scars are fresh from this morning. Plus I don't want to die from getting infected.

Maybe from pi-

Stop.

Okay. So the plan is that I call my brother and then I'll talk to Zach and tell him I don't want to be in a relationship with him and then he'll probably think I used him.

Great.

Tears start to form in my eyes again but I don't let them escape. I can do this.

I take the last look in the mirror and leave the bathroom. Madelin is still passed out on the bed. I put the bottle of vodka in my bag and get out of there. I quickly walk out of the house and then turn on my phone.

There's a missed call from Alex and two from Zach. I don't think I can talk to Zach right now, so I dial my brother.

He picks up immediately. "Hey, where are you?"

"At Madelin's. Can you pick me up?" I try to keep my voice steady.

"Alright, I'll be there right away." He hangs up and I sit down.

It's pretty late but it's still warm. There's a moon, lightening the night sky.

I wait for some time and a car finally stops infront of me. I get up and I'm met with Zachary's stare from the passenger's seat.

This couldn't get any worse, could it?

I open the back door and get in.

"Hey."

"Hi." I say quietly. Zach is looking at me but I can't do anything right now. If what Cade did didn't happen, I would give Zach a kiss on his cheek but I have to keep myself away. Even though it's the last thing I want to do, I have to talk to him tonight.

The drive back is silent, except for Alex who's asking me if I had anything.

"I little." I say shortly.

We get back and I make my way up to my room without saying anything.

"Do you want to eat something?" I hear my brother's voice from behind me.

"Nah, not really."

"Okay." He doesn't look sure though. I think he has noticed there's something wrong.

Zach joins us now and he walks over to me and the only thing I want to do is hug him. I want to get as close to him as I can get but I know I can't so I move away.

Hurt flashes in his eyes and he looks at me questioningly. Alex looks confused as well.

"Zach. Can I talk to you?"

I can see he's worried but he follows me in my room.

We're alone now.

"What's wrong?" He says quietly.

"I can't. I'm sorry. I can't be with you." I spit it out.

He freezes.

"What?" He slowly says.

"I'm sorry, Zach, you have no idea how sorry I am and how much I want it but I can't." I wipe my tears away.

"I- I... what? You're kidding, right?"

I don't say anything.

I can see when the realisation kicks in and he breaks down. I've never seen him cry before and now I am. There are tears falling down his cheeks because of me. I made him cry.

He sorts himself out. "Why?"

"I just can't."

"Okay." Zach slowly nods. "Will you ever be able to?"

"I don't know."

I come close to him and kiss his cheek. "I'm so sorry."

He looks at me and kisses my forehead and then he's out of here.

And I'm alone. All alone. And I totally break down.

Why am I keep hurting people? My mom and now Zachary.

I get in my bed and cry my eyes out. Why does it hurt so much?

Someone knocks and slowly opens my door. When Alex sees me, he quickly runs to me and sits down beside my lying body. My dirty used body.

"Are you okay?" He asks and pulls some strands of my hair away from my face.

I nod. "I just had to. I'm so sorry." He sadly smiles at me.

"You don't have to keep pushing people away, Valeri. We are here for you, okay?"

"I know. I just want to be alone right now." I whisper.

Alex hugs me and leaves.

I'm alone again and it's my fault this time.

AN: -word count- 1671

I'm so sorry for this but I had to:(

I'm really tired because it's 2AM so I'll just go to sleep.

I love u! Night<3

"No it's not. Oh shit, if I could take it back I would."

"No, it's alright."

He sighs and ruffles my hair. "I'm going out. I've got work."

"Where to?"

"At a restaurant. Twenty minutes away." He says.

"Is he going with you?"

"Zach? No, not today. And it's just a summer job, so it isn't that important. It's almost four and my shift finishes at eight. Zach will drive you to the restaurant and we'll all eat something there, okay?"

"Are you kidding me?"

"What?"

"This will be a constant reminder to Zach." He still doesn't get it. "I broke up with him last night, Alex."

"Oooohhh. Makes sense. I'm sorry. But you can't ignore him forever. He's literally living with us."

"I know." I slump back on my bed.

"You'll be there at eight?" He asks.

"Yes, of course. I'll see you later, then."

He smiles at me. "Yeah." And he's gone.

Today will be hell.

ZACHARY

Alex has just invited me and Valeri to the restaurant. I'm wondering how she's doing.

She didn't tell me why she ended things between us but I'm assuming it's what she's struggling with.

I'm not mad and I know she needs space. However, I could be there for her. And a few hours before, she was totally fine. She kissed me and then later she came home and just blew me off.

I don't know what's going on. I will have to ask her.

VALERI

It's half past seven and I got ready to go out. I'm facing Zach for the first time after you know what.

Every time I move, I feel pain all over my body. My whole left side hurts. Yup, I'm right-handed.

I take a pill for my nerves. I've run out of painkillers yesterday.

Fuck, I must text Ryan for more.

I open the drawer and put all the things out until I finally find my burner phone. I turn it on and scroll to Ryan's contact.

Me: I need more.-v

I put it my bag, next to other things and leave my bedroom.

I'm dressed in some baggy black jeans and a sweater.

I find Zach in the living room. He looks up when he sees me and I notice sadness on his face. And then I realise that I'm the one who caused it.

He must have been waiting for me, because he seems ready.

He stands up and clears his throat. "How are you?"

"Good." I can hear my voice sounds hollow.

"Good." He nods and heads to the car. I follow him.

We're in it now. Zach is driving and I'm sitting next to him.

We're silent most of the ride until I break it. "I want us to be friends."

"We are."

"I know, but I want us to be as close as we were before." I know I'm a bitch for saying this, because I was the one who broke up with him in the first place.

He grips the steering wheel. "Why? Why did you do it?"

"Because I had to."

"Yeah, but why did you have to?"

"You don't get it." I whisper.

"Of course I don't get it. You won't tell me."

I close my eyes. "Forget it. I'm sorry for doing it. It was the last thing I wanted to do."

Zach nods. "I want to be there for you. And I will be."

We get out of the car and go in the restaurant.

Alex joins us after a couple of minutes. "So, what do you want to eat?"

We are done eating now, even though I left almost everything on my plate. They don't say anything about it and I'm grateful for it.

"I'll just use the bathroom before we go."

"Alright." Alex says.

I find it and enter. I lock myself in one of the stalls and sit down on the toilet. I turn on my burner phone and look at the messages.

Unknown(Ryan): Midnight. You know where to find me.

I guess I'll be sneaking out of the house tonight.

AN: -word count- 1539

There will be so much drama soon and I can't wait to write it. I don't think I'll publish another chapter for a few days because of school, but I'll see. Maybe I'll even post another today.

Don't forget to vote and comment;)

Have a great day

-j

21

- -

It's 11.30PM and Alex and Zachary went to their rooms. I don't think they're asleep yet, but Ryan said to meet him at midnight. I have half an hour left to get to his house.

I put both of my phones in my bag and take some money and slowly open my bedroom door. Zach and Alex are just across the hallway so I have to be quiet.

The house is silent and the only light that is turned on is above the stairs. I slowly move down them.

If they hear me, I just hope they'll think I'm getting something to drink.

Okay, I made it downstairs now. I walk down another hallway and get to the door. There's a key in it and I slowly turn it to the left.

I step out, take the key and my shoes with me and lock the door. I just hope they aren't going to check on me.

I look around. It's pretty dark. The street lights are the only sources of light here. I put the keys in the pocket of my bag and check the time.

11.40PM

I can make it.

I put on my shoes and walk over the driveway until I come to the road. I haven't been outside by myself here before.

Ryan didn't have to text me his address because I saw him yesterday infront of his house. I know where it is.

I step on the sidewalk and start walking. I keep turning around because of my anxiety. It feels like someone's following me but I know there's no one. Plus I'm scared of the dark.

I walk slowly because I have time. A few minutes later I see his house. I can see that its walls aren't freshly painted from here. But it doesn't look bad.

I cross the street and here it is. Infront of me. I check the time again.

11.55PM

I move away from the street lights and take out my burner phone. I find his contact and text him.

Me: I'm outside

I walk up the stairs until I come to his front door. I wait for some time and then it finally opens.

He doesn't open the door completely. Just enough that I can slip in.

And I do.

Ryan closes the door behind me and goes to what looks like a kitchen.

I'm choosing between following or waiting but then I pick the first choice.

The light in the kitchen is on, so I look around.

"Same like last time?" Ryan speaks.

"No, just painkillers, if you have any." He looks at me.

"Sure." He leaves the room and comes back a few minutes later. "Here." He puts some on the counter.

I take the money out of my bag until i remember. "Do you maybe have something stronger? To help me sleep."

"I only have Rohypnol. You know it?"

Yeah I do. I remember mom taking it and I also know it's the most common used drug for rape.

"Yes." But I don't know if I should take it. I guess I can buy it and not use it. Just in case I ever need it. "I'll take it."

"This shit isn't good, V." Ryan warns me. Isn't he the one who offered it to me?

"I know. I'm not sure if I'll take it but maybe I'll need it."

"Okay. How many?"

"I don't know. Ten?"

"Okay. It'll cost you a bit more." I put some more money on the counter. "Take only one. It won't end well if you take more. I honestly don't know if it was a good idea I told you this."

He slides all the pills to me and takes the money. I put them in my bag and look around.

I can see the living room from here. There's a couch and opened TV. There's a small table in the middle and I can clearly see the white powder.

Fuck. I want to try.

Stop.

Ryan seems to notice and goes to stand at the door, so I can't see it. "I don't recommend."

"Why not?"

"It's too dangerous."

"I know. My mom overdosed with it."

"Is she okay?"

"She's dead."

"Oh." He looks at me shocked. "I'm sorry for your loss. How long ago was it?"

"Around three weeks." I say. I was one week here before we went on two week vacation. "You know, I always said I'll never be like her, but look at me now. Something bad happens to me and I'm already turning to drugs."

He's quiet.

I grab my bag. "Well, I guess I'll go now." And then I stop. "Or maybe I could stay?" I look around his shoulder.

He stares at me. "If you want to. I'm not giving you any of it though."

"Why? When we met at the party, you asked me if I wanted some."

"I thought you've done it before."

I think for a bit and sigh. "Alright. Can I still stay? For an hour or two? I can't risk my brother seeing me sneak back into the house. I'm lucky if he hasn't found my empty bed yet."

"Sure, you can stay here for some time." Ryan leads me into living room. He cleans the table and tells me to sit down on the couch.

I drop my bag on the floor and make myself comfortable.

He brings me a glass of water and sits down beside me.

"So. What do you want to talk about?" He asks.

"I don't know. Anything."

"Why do you want to start? You said you don't want to be like your mom was." He wonders.

I just don't think I will be here for much longer.

"I don't know. I've been feeling down for two weeks. I mean I've never been okay, you know, this with my mom and other things."

"You have Alex now, don't you? And Zach? I saw you two together."

"I broke up with him last night."

"Oh really?"

"Yup. We were together for only a week."

"Wow."

I shove him with my elbow.

Ryan leaves the room and returns with some weed.

It didn't end well the last time.

But I don't care anymore. I don't give a fuck about anything.

He takes a drag and offers it to me.

"You're letting me do this and not that?" I shake with my head and inhale it.

I lean back and close my eyes.

This is it.

I take another and give it back to Ryan. We switch it until it consumes me. Why does it feel so good?

I stare at him and he looks at me.

"Your eyes are red as fuck. Was it too much?" I looks like it didn't affect him as much as it affected me.

I giggle. This shit feels great. I missed this feeling.

Ryan helps me drink some water but I spill half of it.

"Fuck, V."

"How will you go home like this?" He says under his breath.

My laughing turns into tears. Ryan strokes my hair back and I wish it was Zach. I wish I could curl up next to him in his bed and he would play with my hair like usually. But I know this will never be able to happen. I lost my chance with him. I broke his heart and I don't think he will ever want me back. I fucked up. Why do I always fuck everything up?

"What's wrong, V?"

I sit up. "Everything. I can't do this anymore, Ryan." I look at him through my tears.

"Ey, it's okay. You're feeling down. You said it has happened before. It will be better."

"Not this time. I don't think I can do it this time."

"You can. I believe in you, V." He says.

I start calming down and get up. "I should go back." I grab my bag and turn away.

"Let me walk you home." I hear Ryan say and we both leave the house. Cold air helps me clear my head.

He grabs my forearm and I flinch back. "Sorry." He apologises.

"It's okay." I nod at him and we continue walking. We stay in the shadows so no one can see us.

We soon reach my house and I turn to Ryan. "Thanks. For the..." I look at my bag. "And for walking me home."

He nods and I turn around and quietly unlock the house. Before I get in I turn around and see Ryan go back home.

I sigh and put off my shoes and slowly walk up the stairs. I still feel a bit dizzy because of the weed but I'm better.

I close my bedroom door behind me and go in the bathroom. I undress and take a quick shower because I have to clean the smell of everything off me. I put on some underwear and Zach's shirt that he let me borrow a few days ago. Everything Ryan gave me will stay hidden behind my clothes. I take a painkiller and two sleeping pills. I shove Rohypnol behind everything, keeping it there if I ever need it.

AN: -word count- 1528

This is my third update today, so there won't be one for a couple of days.

Don't forget to vote and comment!

I love u, byee

-j

22

- -

"No please don't."

"Don't what?" He says as he pushes me back on the bed.

I quickly get up but his friend is there too. He takes me into his arms and pushes me back down.

They both tower over me.

"Please don't." I beg as Cade lifts up my dress. I hit his hand but it doesn't help.

"Don't make a sound or it'll be so much worse." He threatens.

I have to find Alex or Zach. Anyone.

I know what's about to happen so I do the only thing Cade told me not to do.

I yell for Alex.

I immediately regret it as his hand finds its way to my face.

I don't hear anything. And I can't say anything because his friend's palm is now covering my mouth.

I can hear someone unbuckling his belt but I keep my eyes shut.

"You're doing great, baby. Don't move." I can feel him now. His hot breath is on my cheek and I feel like throwing up.

I feel him thrust inside and tears sting my eyes. I try to push him off but someone is holding my legs and I know their hands will leave bruises.

He's rough. I can't fight anymore so I just lie there staring at the door with hope that someone will come looking for me.

I wake up in sweat. I try to cuddle up next to Zach.

But no one is here.

The realisation hits me.

So I just lie back down hugging my pillow as if it was Zach.

The pills didn't completely work.

I breathe in the smell of Zach's shirt that I'm wearing but it isn't the same. He should've been here, next to me, but I fucked up.

I try to sleep again but I can't. I move around for probably around an hour or more trying to find a comfortable position. After some more time I give up.

I open the drawer and take out more sleeping pills. I pour them on my palm and swallow them all.

They should work.

I don't want to try Rohypnol because if Alex or Zach find me asleep and try to shake me awake, I'm going to end up in hospital. Plus it's only a few hours until morning.

I slide back in bed and close my eyes. I can feel them slowly kick in. It takes a while, but when it does, I fall into a dreamless sleep.

~~~

A painful headache wakes me up the next morning, but I don't have the energy to actually get out of bed.

I don't have energy to do anything, so I just lie there.

A few memories from last night come back. Ryan. Weed. Pills.

At the thought of break up with Zach, I cover my head with a blanket and try to fall asleep again.

ZACHARY

It's evening and Valeri didn't come out of her room all day. Alex went to check up on her and said that she isn't feeling alright.

He left for work a few hours ago and left me home with his sister. I haven't seen her since yesterday's dinner and I'm trying to stay away, because she broke up with me, so I'm assuming she doesn't want to be in my presence.

Although I'm worried, I try to give as much space as she needs.

Alex told me to check up on her every few hours and that means I must go see her now.

I make my way upstairs and stop at her door. I listen but I don't hear anything, so I softly knock, scared I'll wake her up if she's by any chance sleeping.

I don't hear her move so I open the door. Her room is dark. The only source of light is coming from outside where it isn't completely dark yet.

The only thing I hear is her slow breathing. I look around and realise she hasn't eaten anything since last night. No surprise she's been sleeping the whole day.

I turn the light on.

I see Valeri lying on her bed, facing the window, so I can't see her face. Her dark hair are sprawled over the pillow her head is lying on and she's covered with a sheet and a blanket.

A plate with food is on her nightstand. I can see it from the door, Valeri hasn't touched it yet.

I step closer and it looks like she hears me, because she moves around and faces me. She's blinking fast, probably surprised by the light.

I can see Valeri freeze when she notices me standing in the middle of her room.

VALERI

The sudden light wakes me up. How long have I been sleeping? I hear someone at the door. Panic consumes my body and I quickly turn around and freeze when I notice Zach standing at my door.

"Hey," he says after he clears his throat.

"Hey," I mutter as I sit up. I know I look like shit because I feel like shit.

"How are you feeling?"

How am I feeling?

"I want to be alone." I tell Zach.

I notice he's wearing sweats and a black t-shirt. My eyes travel upwards until they reach his face. I'm surprised when I see worry written all over it, because I thought he hated me for ending our relationship without a reason.

He told me last night that we're of course still friends, but I thought he said it out of pity.

"You didn't eat anything today, Valeri. You have to."

"I'm not hungry." I say quietly looking at the food on my nightstand.

"There's no way you're not hungry." He doesn't give up. "You barely ate anything at the restaurant last night." He closes the door and sits down on my bed.

I cover my head with a blanket so he doesn't see my tears that are threatening to fall down my cheeks.

I feel his hand trying to move it away and he wins. Zach uncovers my face and looks down at me.

"Alex said you're not feeling okay. What's wrong?" He asks.

I shrug with my shoulders and touch my tangled hair.

"Nothing. Just... you know... everything." I look away.

His eyebrows furrow at my words. "You wanna talk?" He asks.

I shake with my head.

"Can I ask you something?" He asks and I nod.

"Why did you... you know... end it?" Zach asks.

Maybe because our friend's cousin and his friend raped me and when I finally thought, he was going to leave me alone, he threatened me to break up with you for no reason?

He starts unbuckling his pants. "This is your last chance to say yes. To say that you'll do as I told you to, otherwise you know what is going to happen."

I'm sorry Zach, my love, but I can't go through this again...

It takes me a few seconds but I finally spit it out. "Yes, I'll do as you said."

"What are you going to do?"

"I'm going to break up with him."

"If I find out you're lying, I'll tell every single one of your friends that you're buying from Ryan and that we had sex because you were so desperate for it. And me and Marc will find you and do it again and again until you do listen to us, you understand? Maybe we'll even invite someone else with us." He smirks down at me. I blink the tears away and I hear him put on his belt again and I sigh out. "You're a slut. Don't forget that." He kisses my neck hard and I know he's going to leave a hickey.

Then he gets off me and leaves the room with a slam of the door.

I close my eyes and pull at my hair. The flashbacks ends but I can still see his eyes looking at me.

"Valeri, what's wrong? Valeri?" I lift my head up and look at Zach. I forgot he was here with me.

"What's wrong? What was that?" Zach asks his voice shaking.

"You need to leave."

He looks taken aback but I can still clearly see his curious expression.

"What?"

"I want to be alone. Can you leave?" I mutter.

He slowly stands up. "Okay."

I thought he was going to be mad but instead, I can hear sadness in his voice.

I'm sorry. I'm sorry for hurting you. If I could take everything back, I would have already.

The word stay unspoken when he leaves my room and I'm alone again. I hurt him. I hurt him. I hurt him.

I pull the sheet over my face and silently sob into it.

"And me and Marc will find you and do it again and again until you do listen to us, you understand? Maybe we'll even invite someone else with us." He smirks down at me.

I close my eyes shut wishing I could keep him outside of my head.

However, that isn't possible.

AN: -word count- 1502

I'm sorry for not updating. It was because of school.

What do you think? Will Valeri get better? Is pushing Zach away the right thing to do? Wait and find out in the next few chapters.

I decided there will be 30 to 35 chapters. Do you think it's enough or is the story too short? Because I don't know how to feel about it. I alr know how the story will end but I don't think I can make it to 40 chapters or more.

Don't forget to vote and comment!

Byee

-j

23

- -

A LEX

I don't know what's going on with my sister. I barely see her through the day. She's always in her room, doesn't eat and sleeps all the time.

It's been a week since she came out of her room and I'm honestly freaked out.

I can see Zach is worried as well. He told me what happened when he went to see her. I wonder if she is doing something other than sleeping.

Something is wrong.

VALERI

I've been lying in my bed the whole week high on pills. They're the only things that can help me right now. That keep me calm.

They keep flashbacks and bad memories away. They help me feel nothing.

Alex and Zach kept coming in my room but I didn't speak. I ate a bit but not much.

I'm moving around my bed trying to calm down but I can't. I let out a loud sigh.

And now I think I need alcohol.

I move over and reach under my bed. I touch for a bottle that I took from Madelin last week. It takes me some time but I finally grab it.

I sit up and look around. Painful headache is pounding my head but I hope alcohol will help it.

I open it and take a sip. Although it's burning my throat as I swallow it, I don't stop.

I put it down after a few more sips and stumble to the bathroom. I turn on the shower and step under the water with my clothes still on.

I want to feel something other than sadness, anger and pain. At the same time I want to stay numb. I think it's better than that.

Water consumes my clothed body, my face, my hair, the cuts on my arms. I lean on a wall and slowly sit down putting my hair our of my face. I look around and spot the blade I've been hurting myself with. I lift up my shirt with shaking hands and look at my body. The cuts on my ribs healed but not fully. I'm assuming they won't turn white but red and purple. I think they will stay there forever.

I place the weapon on the left side of my stomach and pull it across my skin. I have to cover my mouth with my other hand to not yell out.

Hot tears leave my eyes and mix with pouring water. I look down and see red joining them. I squeeze my fist together with the blade between my palm and fingers. It cuts me deep and I drop it and look at my hand.

Fuck.

I turn off the water and crawl out of the shower, on cold tiles. I open a drawer and pull out a towel. I put it over my hand and another one on my stomach. I keep it there for some time until I see blood stop.

I look at my palm. A red line is decorating it and blood is slowly coming out of it.

I pull my wet clothes off my wet body.

I press the towel back on my palm and search for bandages. I wrap one around my palm and then clean the new fresh cuts on the side of my stomach.

6 years ago...

I was doing my homework at my house with Zach. We met a few years ago when he moved here with his parents. They were moving quite a lot because of their work but they are still here.

Zach is sitting next to me drawing a picture for art class. He was never really good at it, but I always hyped him up.

He was drawing a tree when the pencil fell out of his hand onto the floor. He jumped off his chair and picked it up. He tried to continue drawing but realised the pencil point broke.

I opened my drawer and took out a sharper.

"Here." I offered it to him and he smiled at me with his dimples I always adored.

"Thanks." He took it and started sharping the broken pencil. I looked at it but quickly pulled my gaze off it.

I continued writing my maths homework when Zach's phone started ringing.

"It's my mom." He said and picked it up.

The phone call was short and then he told me he needs to go home for dinner.

"I will bring you some, okay? I will be back in half an hour." He got off his seat and I followed him.

He pulled his arms around me. "You don't have to." I said.

"Yes, I do. You can't go to sleep without eating." He convinced me.

"Okay. I'll see you later then." I gave him a smile and he left my room.

After I heard the front door shut I opened the drawer and took it out. A sharper.

I looked it over. I've never done it before, but the urge to hurt was growing. I took out scissors and put the blade off. It took me at least ten minutes but I finally did it.

I sat down on the floor leaning my back on the side of my bed.

I pulled up my sleeve.

Should I do it?

Just a tiny cut and I will never do it again.

I pressed it down and slowly slid it across my forearm. Pain shot through it and I had to close my eyes. A tear left my eye causing them to open.

There was nothing at first, but then the line turned red and I felt relieved. Why did I feel relieved?

I put it on again and repeated it. Soon there were five cuts, not just one.

I sat on my bedroom floor for sometime, looking at my blood dripping out of the cuts I made.

I was so caught up into it that I didn't hear my bedroom door open. I quickly looked up and saw Zach frozen infront of me.

I stood up as fast as I could and squeezed the blade in my arm.

"Wha- what? What did you do?" Zach stood infront of me looking down at my arm.

The worry on his face made more tears come out of my eyes making my vision blurry.

He rushed to me and pulled me into a hug. I just stood there frozen in place.

What did I do?

Zach pulled away and looked down at me. "It's okay. I've got you." He took my hand and led me in the bathroom.

PRESENT

More tears fall at the memorie. If he saw me now. How stupid and broken I am.

I don't know what I'm doing. I have no idea what am I still doing here. I am a disappointment. A disappointment to Alex and my Zach. To all of them.

I stand up and put some clothes on me. I leave the bathroom without looking in the mirror or anything and go to the drawer. I open it and as I'm reaching for Rohypnol to end it all, a loud knock interrupts my intentions.

I let out a sigh of relief. I don't know if I'm mad or grateful for the person that is at the door.

I wasn't seriously going to do it, was I?

It was only a thought.

Just a thought.

I shut the drawer and approach the door. I look at myself in the mirror and then open it.

Alex is standing infront of me.

"Hey." He says.

"Hi." I mutter.

"I heard the shower running. I see you finally got out of bed. Are you better now?" He asks.

Am I better? No. I'm worse than I ever was in my life, but I don't have to show him that, right?

I can pretend I'm okay for some more time, a few more days maybe, but then...

"Yeah, I'm still not feeling great but I'm better."

"It's good to hear." He smiles at me and pulls me in his embrace.

I hold onto him silently thanking him for seeing him.

"Come down for dinner, okay? You won't have to eat all of it. Just a little." My brother reassures me when I pull away.

I nod at him. "I'll be downstairs in a few minutes, okay?"

He smiles at me and leaves the room.

I exhale. Fuck. Alright, I can do it.

I open the door and make my way to the stairs. I stop when I see Zach walking up.

I take a few steps but then I stumble. Black colors my vision and I have to hold onto the railing so I don't fall down.

Zach grabs my arm with one hand and my waist with the other. "Are you okay?" He asks.

"Yeah, of course." I take a deep breath and continue walking. Zach follows me close behind until I sit down at the table. Alex is already there, waiting for us.

Zach sits down next to me and we start eating.

Little do they know this is one of our last dinners together.

I just don't think I can do it for much longer.

AN: -word count- 1521I can't read it through again because I'm half asleep, so there might be some writing mistakes.

Bye!

-j

24

V ALERI

Madelin

Madelin: Down for a party? Ayna, Mers and others will be there too. Ask Alex and Zach if they wanna come.

Me: ofc when

Madelin: 9PM

Me: alr

She texts me an address. I put my phone down and roll on my back.

It's 8pm now.

I stand up and rub at my eyes. I need a shower. I take some clothes and turn on the fifth shower today. I tried to clean off their touch but it didn't go away.

When I'm done I put on some basketball shorts-as usual, a croptop and a zip up. I look in the mirror and brush my long hair. I do myself an eyeliner and when I'm satisfied with my look I get back in my bedroom. I take some painkillers. It's like a habit now, I guess?

I take my bag and put everything I need in it.

I check the time. 8:30pm.

I glance up and stare at the wall. Everything is so distant now. It doesn't feel real. Do you know this feeling when you look down at your hands and realise you're a counscous mind living in a body?

I've been feeling like this for quite a lot of time now. Especially the last four days since I ate dinner with my brother and Zach.

I sigh and lie back. I stare at the ceiling and wish...

Wish I could go back or wish nothing has ever happened. Wish I would wake up everyday with a smile on my face thinking it's another day.

But it's right the opposite now. Most of the time I wish I wouldn't wake up at all. I just want to be in that unknown darkness. In peace. I wish I could stay there forever.

I wish i could sleep forever. Without dreams. Be unconscious, when you don't even know you're alive, a living creature.

Yeah well, I'm still alive, aren't I?

I close my eyes and breathe in. I pull at my hair.

I look at my phone. 8:47pm.

I need to go downstairs.

But why is it that hard to get up? Why does it have to be so hard? It's like my mind freezes. Like I'm on the edge of standing up but it feels like my mind won't let me.

Okay, I must get downstairs.

I finally pull myself up, take my bag and leave my room. I walk down the stairs and see Alex and Zach talking in the living room.

"Where are you going?" My brother asks.

"Out with others. Madelin said you two should come too, if you want."

I see them look at each other. "Sure. Give us a minute."

ZACHARY

I love her.

That's why I'm giving her space, as she asked me to.

I just wish I could hear that laugh again and play with her hair while she's falling asleep.

We're at the party now. Me and Alex were surprised Valeri wanted to go, because she was staying in her room all the time.

But I can see Alex is relieved. And I am too.

~~~

"What's up with Valeri? We haven't seen her for like ten or eleven days" Lach says.

Valeri left to get something to drink a few seconds ago and we are sitting on a couch talking.

"Yeah, like I haven't seen her since she took that pregnancy test last week. She was so freaked out. And was so relieved when it turned out negative. And then she just disappeared." Madelin says.

A pregnancy test? The fuck is she talking about?

Everyone looks at me when they hear about what Madelin said.

I'm frozen. We've never...

"When was this? The day she was at yours?" I ask confused.

"Yup, she called me to hang out but then dragged me to the store for some, because she wanted to make sure she's not pregnant. Wait... you didn't know?"

I stare at her in shock. That was the night Valeri broke up with me.

"We've never... " I say when I get my voice back.

"She said that you had... " Madelin looks at me even more confused then I am.

"No- " I shake with my head. "We've never had sex."

In that moment Valeri enters the room.

VALERI

I leave the room because I can't stand looking at Cade anymore. He keeps looking at me with that stupid smirk written on his face. As much as I try to ignore it, I can't. I keep thinking about that night at Madelin's.

I get to the kitchen to find a drink. I pour it into a glass and take a sip.

I stay there for at least ten minutes until I see someone approaching me.

I glance up and freeze with a glass halfway to my mouth.

Before I can move, Cade comes stand right infront of me locking me to the counter with his hands.

I look around and think that he probably won't do anything infront of other people. He won't, right?

I try to put his hand away but he doesn't move.

"I heard you took a pregnancy test last week, didn't you?" He laughs.

I freeze at his words. The glass falls out of my hand on the counter.

"Answer me." He whispers in my ear.

I can't because of shock, so he grips my wrist tight right over my cuts and I flinch, trying to get away from him.

"I won't hurt you if you tell me the truth."

How does he know?

I nod with my head.

"Good. Now, listen to me." He grip my jaw until I look at him. "Zach has just found out about it. It slipped out of Madelin's mouth. She thought he knew it, you know? How stupid of her. How stupid of you to bring her to the store with you."

Cade laughs. "You'll do as I say, again. You know what is going to happen otherwise or should I repeat it?"

"What do you want from me?" I spit out.

"You'll go back there, where everyone is and when Zachary asks you to tell him the truth, you know what will you say? That you cheated on him. I will be there. I will watch you and listen to everything you say."

No no no no no no

I can't hurt Zach like that.

"You understand?"

I slowly nod, because I can't fight Cade anymore. I'm not able to do anything.

"Come there in two minutes." Cade kisses my neck and I look away, tears threatening my eyes.

Cade steps away from me and goes back to the room where everyone is.

Okay. I can do it.

Just a few more days, Valeri. You can do it. You'll be free then.

I gulp down another drink and go back.

He hates you already for what you did. You are selfish.

I step in the room and all of my friends look at me.

It's okay. I'll be gone soon.

"Valeri."

"Hey, something wrong?"

"A pregnancy test, really?" Zach stands up.

I freeze. Cade wasn't lying.

I look at my left. My rapist's eyes are staring back at me as he slowly nods.

"What?" I mutter.

"You know what." He seems hurt. "I understand that you ended things but that you... that you cheated?"

I shake with my head. This can't- this can't be happening. I don't want to do this.

"Just tell me the truth, Valeri. Did you cheat?"

I stare at him in shock.

I can see Cade nodding from the left and I know I have to do it.

"I'm sorry." I'm sorry for hurting you.

I can see the last sparks of hope die in his eyes.

"I'm sorry. I'm so sorry." I sit down on the couch with my head in my hands.

"I didn't mean to."

"What do you mean you didn't mean to?" He quietly asks.

"It just happened. I'm sorry." I look at him.

"Alright." He's quiet. "I'm out of here." Zach rushes out of the room.

I sob in my hands. I can't do this shit anymore.

I feel everybody's eyes on me. I get up and leave.

AN: -word count- 1361

This chapter is a bit shorter but it took me a lot of time to write it.

How are you?

What do you think will happen?

Don't forget to vote and comment!

Bye

-j

25

ZACHARY

I honestly don't know what to do. I didn't believe when Madelin said what she said. But then, when Valeri told me that she cheated...

I don't know.

I've never imagined Valeri being like that. I've never thought she would do that.

Until now.

I needed to get some air, so I went outside. And now I'm here sitting on the stairs behind the house.

She admitted.

As much as I don't want to believe it, she admitted she has done it.

I'm deep in my thoughts when I feel a hand on my shoulder.

"Zach." I immediately recognize my best friend's voice.

Alex sits down beside me and hugs me.

"I can't believe it." I admit.

"I know. Me neither." He says quietly.

"I've known her since forever. I never thought she was capable of doing that."

"I know. It's okay. I'll text Madelin to find her and drive her home. Come on, let's go." Alex helps me up and we walk around the house until we get to the car. We get in and Alex drives us home.

We are quiet the whole ride until we pull on the driveway. We walk up the stairs without saying anything.

I get upstairs to my room and take a quick shower. When I'm done, I go back downstairs.

Alex is in the kitchen talking to someone on the phone. He looks stressed out.

"What's wrong?"

He quickly looks at me but focuses back on the phone. "Should I come get her?... no?... okay... thanks." He puts the phone on the table.

"What happened?"

"Uhh... nothing. Madelin found Valeri on a random bench in the middle of nowhere and she's bringing her home."

"Oh."

"Yeah, she's blacked out."

I nod.

"Are you okay with her being here?"

"Yeah I mean it's her house, not mine." I reassuringly smile at him.

We both sit down and wait.

MADELIN

The shit went down. Although I feel like I fucked up, Zach finally found out the truth. We all did.

I don't know what to say. It's not what I expected. Valeri lied about it.

And it's unfair to Zach. He's a really good person and I thought he finally got someone who deserved him, but now...

A text interrupts my thoughts.

Alex: can you look for Valeri? I know she lied to you, but can you maybe bring her home?

Me: ofc x

Alex: thanks

I put my phone in a pocket and stand up from the couch. Others have already gone home and I'm the only one left here.

I look through every room in the house and when I still don't find her, I step outside.

I notice my cousin sitting outside and as much as I don't like him I approach him. "Have you seen Valeri?"

He stops talking to some people who look pretty high and looks at me.

"Nope. Not since... you know." He smirks and I roll my eyes.

"It's not funny."

"Yeah it is. Seeing Zach like that... " he laughs.

"You're useless." I shove him with my elbow.

I'm turning around when a voice interrupts me. "You're looking for a girl with dark hair and a nose piercing?"

I turn back. It's one of the high looking girls.

"Yeah." I nod.

"Oh. Yeah I saw her. She bought some some of this..." a girl points at a bag of white powder. "...and went down the sidewalk that way."

The fuck?

"Thanks." I smile at her and go where she instructed me to.

Valeri buying drugs?

That must be a mistake.

But I have to check there either way.

I walk down the street for some time but I don't see anyone, so I take out my phone and call Valeri.

A sound of a phone scares me. I hear phone ringing a few metres away. It can't be a coincidence, can it?

I move closer to the sound until I come to a park. It's coming from one of the benches. I look there and see a person sitting on the floor leaning their back on a side of the bench.

Fuck. It's Valeri.

As much as I don't want to see her right now, I know I have to make sure she's okay and take her home.

I step closer. "Valeri?"

Nothing.

I get closer and kneel down beside her.

"Madelin?" Valeri softly mutters.

"Yeah, it's me, Valeri. We have to go home, now." I tell her.

She starts shaking her head. "No. I cannot. He's there. And my brother."

"I know. I know, but I can't let you stay here. Alex called and he said to bring you home. We need to go." I try to convince her.

That's when I notice an almost empty bottle of alcohol on the bench.

"How much did you drink?" I ask.

She just shrugs with her shoulders, so I take it away. "Come on. We need to go." I grab her under her arms and lift her up and she's now standing on her feet.

Because she's leaning on me, I can barely put her bag over her shoulder. I grab her forearm and help her walk back to my car.

We slowly make it back and I open back door. I push Valeri in, along with her bag and get in the front. Before I start the car, I call Alex.

He answers at the first ring.

"Madelin, hey, did you find her?"

"Yes. On a bench in the middle of nowhere." I tell him.

"Oh wow. Is she okay?"

I look back to find Valeri passed out.

"She's passed out from alcohol. Although I took it from her when I found her, she was already drunk."

"Should I come get her?"

"We're already in the car. We'll be there soon."

"Okay. Thanks." The line goes off and I start the car.

ALEX

A few minutes after the call from Madelin, I hear a car pull in the driveway.

I quickly stand up and look at Zach. He nods at me and I go down the hall toward the front door. I go outside and walk down the stairs to the car and I see Madelin get out of it.

She comes to help me pick Valeri up and then goes back to the front.

"Thank you." I thank her.

"No problem." Madelin smiles at me. "I'll see you tomorrow." She gets back in the car and drives away.

I look down at my passed out sister and take her inside. I walk up the stairs into her room, put her bag on the floor and tuck her in her bed. I turn around to leave but see Zach standing at the door worriedly looking at Valeri.

I turn off the lights and close the door. Zach and I go in my room and sit down on the bed.

It was a long eventful day and I'm drained. I'm sure Zach is too.

"I remember when she literally hit some guy at a party, because he cheated on some girl. She was so mad about it, although it had nothing to do with her."

His words catch me off guard.

"Do you think she regrets it?"

"Yeah, I think so. At least she broke up with me and didn't continue doing it." He sighs.

"You're right, but it's still not okay." I say.

"I still had hope to get her back, but when she admitted what she did..."

We are quiet for some time until he breaks the silence. "Who do you think?" He whispers.

"I don't know." I honestly have no idea. I haven't seen her with any other guy except for my best friend. "Have you seen her with anyone else?"

"Yeah." I glance up at him. "But it was before we've got together. The same night I caught a guy coming out of her room."

"Who?"

"Ryan." He looks at me.

"Ryan?" I'm even more confused now. She and Ryan?

"Yes."

"Oh god." I say under my breath. Another thought catches my mind. "She wanted it with him, right? She gave him consent?"

"I'm not even sure if they did it but we both know Ryan. He's a good person although he has some problems. She looked pretty fine when she came out of her room right after him." He explains and I let out a breath.

"Alex?"

"Ye?"

"Will you check up on her? On how she's doing?" My best friend asks.

I look at him understanding. He's the best person to ever exist and I'm so glad he's my best friend. It pains me seeing him in pain that my sister caused. I love Valeri, but he didn't deserve it. He deserves someone better. He still cares so much about her.

"Of course." I give him a reassuring smile.

"Thanks."

I nod and check the time. It's late and my head is killing me.

"Let's go to sleep."

AN: -word count- 1488

More povs!

I've been sick since Wednesday and I hate it.

The next Wednesday I have a really important exam that affects my future, so I don't know when I'll be able to update.

I'm thinking about writing another book. However, that will probably happen at the end of June, when I finish school. Don't judge me, but I really want to write a mafia book. Ehehehe. Please comment if you're interested!

Don't forget to vote and comment!

Bye.

-j

26

V ALERI

Headache wakes me up the next morning. I open my eyes and am met with my room. I look through the window and see sun shining on the bright blue sky.

I immediately draw the curtains and lie back down.

Sudden memories from yesterday flood my mind and I bury my face in the pillow.

It can't get any worse, can it?

I sigh and close my eyes.

~~~

A few hours later I finally convince myself to get out of bed. I change my clothes and wash my face.

After that, I decide to go downstairs and eat something. I walk down the stairs and enter the kitchen.

I freeze at the sight. They all go quiet.

Fuck. Everybody's here. How could Alex invite them here, knowing what happened yesterday?

I look at the floor and move to the counter and make myself breakfast. They continue their conversation but I can feel their eyes on my back.

I fucked up so bad. I should've told them the truth the day it happened.

But there's no going back now, so I just continue doing myself breakfast.

"How are you, Valeri?" I hear Madelin behind me.

Is she serious or just joking around making fun if me?

"Fine." I quietly say turned away from them. "You?"

"I'm great, thank you." I hear her say.

Although I don't want to, I turn around to look at them.

I see wary expressions on all of their faces. My eyes land on Zach, but he doesn't look at me.

"Thanks for picking me up last night." I say to Madelin.

"I did it for Alex." That hurt, but I can't say I expected them to act like they did before.

"I know." I say. I don't want her to feel like she won.

"Good to know."

I shrug with my shoulders and pour myself some water.

"Was it Ryan?"

I choke on it. "What?"

"Enough, Madelin." I hear my brother warn her. How the fuck do they know anything about Ryan?

"No." I say coldly but I see they don't buy it.

"It doesn't matter, Madelin. It's done." Lach says.

I leave the glass on the counter and exit the kitchen, leaving their voices and judgy looks behind.

What was I expecting?

I should've told them the truth.

But I can't. No one can know about it. Just today and tomorrow and everything is going to go back to normal.

When I enter my room, I climb into my bed and pull a blanket over me. I take a blade from my phone case and put it on my forearm.

There are no tears and no sobs. Only silence filled with my thoughts which are running through my head.

I do a few tiny cuts, roll my sleeve down and then take a piece of paper and a pen. I hold it tightly until my knuckles turn white. I don't wait and start writing one letter to my brother, one to Ayna, Mers, Lach and Kian, one to Madelin and one to Zachary.

Alex, I've had thoughts about suicide in a while now. It was better some days until it wasn't. I've never imagined to actually have a life until I met you. You always understood me and didn't judge me after what you all thought I did. You and your friends made everything better, but it wasn't enough, because something has happened...

...Madelin, you will probably wonder why I'm bringing your cousin, Cade, into this, but he did something horrible. He's been looking at me from the moment I moved here. My brother took me to a party the second night and Cade touched me. I shrugged it off until I realised he's your cousin and I was going to see him again. On vacations, on the night of that first party I went out to get some air. Cade's friend, Marc, drugged me and brought me upstairs to my bedroom. Cade showed up right after that. They locked me in and held me down on the bed and did it. They raped me. Your cousin and his friend raped me. I thought it was over until we came back home and I took you to get a pregnancy test with me. I never cheated on Zach. He was the most amazing person I've ever met in my whole life. Later that night when we went to yours and you fell asleep, Cade entered in the room and pinned me down on the bed and threatened me to break up with Zach or he'd do it again. At the last party, where you thought you knew the truth, you didn't. Cade showed up and threatened me again to say that I cheated, to hurt Zach or something. I don't know why he wanted that. It was too late...

...Zach, I'm sorry I didn't tell you the truth. You don't know how much I wanted, but I couldn't. You saw me with Ryan the night you found out about self harm, the night we first kissed. I want to explain it to you now. I've been self harming since I was younger and after a few years I got addicted to pills. That's why you saw me with Ryan. I was buying from him. He tried to convince me that it isn't worth it, but I did it anyways. It were mostly painkillers and sleeping pills, also Rohypnol with which one I'm going to end my life. Ended my life*. You were the person who brought a spark into me after so many years of hell and I'm grateful for it. Although we were together for only a week, I felt for you so much. You learned me how to feel something other than anger and sadness. I wish we had more time together. I've never said it, but...

I love you, Zachary

-Valeri

I finish writing and realise the paper is now wet from my tears. I quickly put them in envelopes and shut them in my drawer. I cover myself with a blanket over my head. I see blood has soaked through my hoodie, but I don't really care right now. I just want to sleep.

Laughing from the kitchen interrupts me every time I almost drift off. My biggest wish right now was to be down there with my friends and them not hating me.

I swallow two sleeping pills and finally fall asleep.

~~~

I

wake up at 9PM, when someone opens the door in my bedroom. I see it's Alex.

"You didn't respond." He claims.

"I was sleeping." I tiredly say still blinking with my eyes.

He sits down on my bed next to me and puts his arm around my shoulder pulling me closer. "I'm sorry about Madelin."

"It's okay, I deserve it."

"Don't say that." He says looking down at me.

"Why not?"

"No one deserves that."

"I do."

He exhales.

I need to tell him. How do I do that?

I take a deep breath. "Alex, I have to tell you something." He sits up straighter when he hears my tone.

"Is something wrong?" He asks when I don't continue. How do I tell him that everything's wrong. That I want to die.

"I w-was r-"

"Alex where did you go?" A voice interrupts me just as I want to say it.

Someone loudly knocks on the door and opens it. Lach stumbles in my room. "Alex we've been looking for you." Lach stops talking when he notices me.

I quickly look away. To be honest, I don't know if I'm relieved that Lach came here. I almost told my brother. Almost.

I get up from my bed and walk to the bathroom.

"Valeri, what did you want to say?" I hear Alex's voice from behind me.

"It doesn't matter." I shut myself in the bathroom. I instantly start sobbing and tugging my hair. I almost told him the truth. My life almost went back to how it was before. But honestly, I don't think I could do it, although I told him. What happened was too much and there is no way I can continue living like this. Only tomorrow and then it's my 18th birthday and I'll be gone.

I take off my hoodie and look at the cuts I made this morning. My whole hand is bloody and there are old scars all over my wrists and forearms. I want them to notice. I want them to notice I'm not okay.

But they all hate me.

AN: -word count- 1423

This book is so depressed. There's literally not a happy chapter in it. Maybe one or two.

Don't forget to vote and comment!

-j

27

TW: drugs, sh, suicide attempt

VALERI

I've been staring at the wall opposite my bed for the past couple of hours. I lost track of time, but I can tell it's evening. I'm turning eighteen tonight. Or at least I am supposed to.

Others are downstairs, having fun and waiting for Alex to turn eighteen. No one is waiting for me though. My brother came in my room a few times but I didn't say much. He tried to cheer me up but I know he's doing it just because we're related. He thinks of me the same as the others.

I honestly don't know what I'm doing. I can't sleep because of flashbacks, I can't eat because it makes me want to throw up, I can't go downstairs because no one likes me there. They don't want me and they have every right for it.

I took some pills but they don't help me anymore. I'm hopeless and exhausted. I'm done with everything.

I'll go downstairs now. I want to see them one last time. I slowly get up, my body is aching from not eating and from too much pills.

I get to the door and turn the doorknob. I walk down the hall. Their voices get louder. I walk down the stairs and stop.

I take a deep breath and enter.

Everyone looks at me but then continues to act as if I wasn't there.

I don't know what's worse. Madelin saying that yesterday or getting ignored by all of them.

I let out a breath and sit down next to Alex. He smiles at me. I'm going to miss him. "How are you?" He quietly says.

I shrug with my shoulders. "Fine, I guess." I look down at my shaky hands. Not gonna lie, I'm scared.

"I don't see you very often, Valeri. I want to see you more." He says.

For real?

Or is he saying that out of pity?

I nod but I can't look at him. Not with what I'm planning on doing tonight.

I look around the table. Ayna and Mers are holding each other's hands, Lach is annoying Kian. Madelin is staring at me with a wary expression. I look at Zach last. He's talking to my brother and I can't stop looking at him. I wish I could run into his arms. I miss his touch and his reassuring words, his smile and the way he talks. I want to tell him so bad, I don't want him hurting because of me.

"Do you want something to eat?" I shake with my head. "I'm making you something whether you like it or not."

"I'm really not hungry." I say.

He just pats my head and goes to the fridge. I can see other's burning gazes on me now and they make me feel uncomfortable. I shift in my seat and look at the clock.

11:25PM

Half an hour left.

Although I'm scared, I think I'm ready.

Alex puts a plate of pasta infront of me. "I'm not really hungry, Alex."

"Be grateful." I see Madelin roll her eyes. "For a druggie that you are, you should be grateful."

The words cut right through me and it feels like somebody just stabbed my heart. This burning pain in my chest.

"I- I'll go." I quickly stand up and leave the kitchen. Tears are threatening to fall down my cheeks. I'm pathetic for being so emotional. I'm so weak. I run up the stairs, although I hear someone following me.

"Valeri." My brother calls me. He grabs my wrist so I turn around and look at him. Tears have already spilled down my face and I can't seem to stop them.

"It's okay. I'm sorry she said that." He hugs me and I squeeze him back but then pull away. "She's right though." I take one last look at him, and then shut myself in my room. I slide down the door and sob in my hand. After some time I hear him go back downstairs.

I slowly stand up.

What Madelin said was my last reason. It wasn't the problem that she said that, but that she was right. I'm an addict. I can't stop taking those pills.

My mom was an addict. I guess it runs in a family, although I don't have much of it, anyway.

Who's even going to miss me?

I don't have a mom anymore, my dad isn't present, Alex probably doesn't care about me, because I moved here and got welcomed in a friendgroup which now thinks I betrayed them.

I check the time.

11:45PM

Okay, I'm ready.

I put letters on my nightstand. I hope they'll help them understand every-thing, if they are even going to read it. I open the drawer and take out the Rohypnol. My hand stops above the bag of white powder.

I always wanted to try it. I always wondered why did my mom think the drugs were better than her daughter. I think I should answer my question now.

I take it out and put everything on my bed.

Letters, blade, rohypnol, drugs. I'm ready.

I shake some powder on my nightstand and roll some money.

I want to forget. I want to forget about Cade and Marc, I want to forget about everything.

And I do it.

I cough at first but then my mind goes quiet. And it feels good. So perfect.

I do some more. I kind of get it now.

What have you just done, Valeri?

I overcome the voices by doing it again.

I take the Rohypnol. Ryan said to take one to fall asleep. To bad I don't wanna fall asleep right now.

Although my mind is dizzy and I'm sweating, I take a few. I don't know how many. I don't really care. I swallow them with a glass of water and lie down on my back.

Everything is spinning and I take a blade with my shaky hands slide it across my wrists. I can feel blood start pouring out of the cuts.

The weapon falls out of my palms and when the clock hits midnight, I'm out.

ALEX

When my twin sister came downstairs, it felt like something was off. Maybe I'm overreacting and it was nothing.

I'm mad at Madelin. She has every right for not liking Valeri, but she crossed the line by saying that.

I know it really hurt Valeri. However, she shut herself in her bedroom and I know she wants to be alone.

We're both turning eighteen in five minutes and Lach, Kian, Zach, Madelin, Ayna and Mers are already celebrating.

I want to join them, but something is stopping me. Something feels off. Zach is sitting next to me minding his own business with a drink in his hand.

11:57PM

Three minutes left.

Should I get Valeri? She's probably sleeping though. I'll go wish her happy birthday at midnight. I want to celebrate it together. I'm so happy I met her and spent the last month with her. I'm planning about taking her on a trip. I'm not sure where yet and I would invite Zach with us but after what happened...

11:59PM

"Come on, Alex. One minute left. Have some fun!" Madelin takes my hand and pulls me off couch. I smile at her but I feel something is wrong.

"Ey, I'll check on Valeri. I'll be right back." I explain.

"It's less than one minute left." Madelin argued.

"I'll be right back. I want to celebrate it with my sister first." I get out of the living room and run up the stairs. I approach Valeri's door and softly knock.

When she doesn't respond, I slowly open the door. A lamp on her night-stand is lightening the room.

There's something else though. A white powder is all over it. I look at the left.

Valeri is lying frozen on her bed. I slowly get closer and I already know something is wrong. There's a white powder under her nostrils.

Fuck.

I run up to her and that's when I see it. Red is covering her wrists and the sheets.

I'm frozen in shock.

"Alex? Where did you go?" Zach voice brings me out of my thoughts and I start shaking Valeri awake.

"Valeri, wake up."

Nothing

She doesn't- She doesn't move.

ZACHARY

I went looking for Alex right when it turned midnight. I entered Valeri's room, where I saw him at Valeri's bed.

"Valeri, wake up."

"Please, Valeri."

I come next to him and that's when I see her.

I immediately take a piece of clothing from her chair and start wrapping it around her wrists.

"Alex, call 911."

I hear him look for his phone and start dialing.

Soon the ambulance pulls at the driveway and they start running up to Valeri's room. They say to move away and they'll take care of her.

Alex doesn't move so I have to hold him back, keeping him away from running up to her.

An officer tells us there isn't enough time for Alex to come with her so they leave us in her room.

Everything is blurry, it doesn't feel real. I pull Alex into a hug and he sobs in my shoulder.

"It'll be okay." I whisper. I'm crying myself now.

Valeri, what have you done?

28

·

A LEX

I've been sitting in the hospital for five hours now. The doctors won't let me see my sister, but they said I will see her as soon as possible, if everything goes well.

Zach went out to grab some food. He tried to convince me to go home and get some sleep, but I didn't want to leave Valeri here. Although I have no idea in what state she's in right know, it looked pretty bad when I saw her there lying on her bed unmoving. The white powder under her nose, her cut wrists and the pills on the floor.

I can't forget it. I can't stop the flashbacks. Seeing her like that, on her birthday. Our birthday. This was supposed to be the best birthday of her life, because I know she didn't really celebrate it with her mom. She only celebrated it with Zachary and I'm so grateful for him being there for her when I wasn't.

I feel like I wasn't there for her even after she came to live with me. I wasn't paying enough attention and I'm honestly feeling guilty. I wasn't giving her enough of my time, was I? I noticed she was always in her room, not eating much, being sick all the time but fuck, you don't know how much I wish I could go back and take care of her.

I don't know what made her do it. Maybe the death of her mom or something else.

Right now, I just hope she'll be alright. I believe in her.

The slam of the door brings me out of my thoughts and I look up to see a doctor coming our of Valeri's room. She's a nice middle aged lady with blonde hair and glasses.

"How is she?" I immediately stand up and ask.

"She's stable, but sleeping right now. She overdosed on Rohypnol and cocaine." The doctor sadly looks at me. "She's underweight and shows signs of what looks like self harm."

I stare at a woman infront of me. How could I not see Valeri wasn't okay? Fuck, I should've known. There were so many signs that I missed. She wasn't swimming when we went to the sea, she wore long-sleeved shirts all the time.

I let out a breath.

"When can I see her?" I hopefully asked.

"She probably won't wake up for at least an hour but you're welcome to see her now." She reassuringly smiles at me.

"Okay."

"May I ask where her legal guardian is?" She asks me looking down at the papers in her hand. "We called him, but he said he won't be able to come see her right now."

I completely forgot my father existed.

I clear my throat. "He's on vacation right now, but I believe he'll be back soon."

"Okay. That's all for now. You can go see your sister." The lady nods at me.

"Thank you." She walks down the hall way and I turn to the door. I slowly open it and step inside.

Valeri is lying on her bed. She's sleeping and there are wires connected to her body. She looks pale with dark circles under her eyes. She's wearing a hospital gown, the bandage is wrapped around her wrists.

I come closer. I notice white and red-almost purple-lines all over her arms. I slowly sit down and take her palm into mine.

Valeri looks exhausted. But she's alive. I don't think she'll be happy when she wakes up and realises she failed it. I'm glad she failed. I always wanted a sister or at least a sibling and now that I got her, she almost got away from me.

I care for her so much. I'd take a bullet if it meant she was safe. I bring her hand up and kiss it.

Why did you do it?

I hope she will be comfortable opening up to me, but I shouldn't keep my hopes up, because if she didn't tell me before, she probably won't tell me now. However, I'll make sure she finds a person she can truly trust.

The door of the room opens and Zachary storms in with a bag of food. He looks tired and I probably look like shit as well. We haven't slept for almost twenty four hours.

He drops the food on a chair on the other side of the room and quickly comes closer. "Oh fuck, is she going to be okay?

I nod. "Yeah, she's okay now." I look down at my sleeping sister and sadness and guilt overcomes my body. I feel anger as well for whoever made her do it. For the reason she tried to end it all.

I trail my fingertips over her healed scars and a tear escapes my eye. "She harms herself." I whisper.

Zach sits next to me, puts his arm over my shoulder and pulls me close. "Did she tell you she still does it when you were together?"

ZACHARY:

Alex looks me in the eyes and there's no way I can lie to my best friend.

"Yeah, I knew." I truthfully tell him. "But she didn't want you to be worried, so she asked me not to tell you."

He nods. "I'm just so sad she wasn't enough comfortable to do that."

I hug him.

My biggest wish was that Valeri wouldn't end up like that. Like her mom did. That was her wish as well. I don't know what made her do it. Guilt? Grief?

"She will be okay." I whisper to Alex.

"I hope so."

That's when Valeri stirs awake. Alex quickly takes her hand and hopefully looks at her.

She slowly opens her eyes and blinks a few times because of bright lights. She's so fucking beautiful. Although she looks pale and tired, she's the prettiest woman I've ever seen.

"Where am I?" Her voice is hoarse but it's still like music to my ears.

Shut up, Zach.

You shut up.

"Hey, Valeri." Alex softly says. "How are you feeling?"

"Terrible." She doesn't look at us. I see panic in her eyes. I see that the fact that she failed, sank in.

The door opens again and the doctor comes in.

"I see you're awake, honey." She smiles at Valeri. But my best friend's sister just looks at her.

"When can I go home?" Valeri asks.

"In the afternoon."

"Okay."

"I'll come check again in a couple of hours." The doctor says and leaves, so now it's just me, Alex and Valeri here.

Right after we found Valeri, Kian, Lach, Madelin, Ayna and Mers left. We told them we'll call them later.

VALERI

I failed. I fucking failed. I literally did everything I could to end it, and I didn't succeed.

Embarrassing.

My body feels weak and my head hurts. Alex and Zach are sitting next to my bed and talking to each other while I'm trying to sleep.

It's 4PM now. I can leave in an hour.

Have they read the letters I left? A part of me hopes they have, but the other is embarrassed.

I want to tell them though. When we get home.

"Alex? Did you two read the note I left?" They stop talking and look at me.

"No, we rushed here right away and we weren't sure if you'd still want us to read it." Zach explains.

I wish he had read it. "Oh, okay. Everything is explained in it."

They curiously look at me but don't say anything because I told them I don't want to talk about it right now.

The hour goes by very quickly and I'm getting ready to go home. Alex brought me some clothes that I changed into. He had to help me because my body is still weak. The doctor gave me some food but it tasted horrible and I didn't have much appetite, so I barely ate anything. Zach promised he'll cook something when we get home.

We're sitting in a car right now. Zach is driving and my brother is in the back with me. The ride home is silent and I'm so happy when we enter the house. I was already sick of the hospital.

"I can walk." I tell Zach for the fifth time now but he doesn't listen.

I'm suddenly lifted up in the air. Zach has one hand under my knees and the other one under my back. I hold onto him as he walks up the stairs. We make it to Alex's room and he puts me down on the bed.

Zach stands up to go downstairs to cook something but I stop him. "Why do you care about me? You haven't read the letter yet. You still think I cheated." He looks at me with furrowed eyebrows.

"Because no one deserves whatever you went through." He tells me. "Hold on. What's written in the letter?" He wonders.

Alex enters the room with a plate full of pancakes. I guess Zach doesn't have to go downstairs now.

My brother puts the food next to me and I look back at Zach. "Can you get the letters for me? They're in my room on the bedside table."

"Sure." Zach leaves and Alex sits down next to me. He takes a pancake and bites into it. "Take one." He demands.

I can't.

Zach saves me when he returns with four letters in his hand. "These?"

I nod and give him his. I put the other one to my brother.

"Are you sure you want us to read it?"

"Yeah, otherwise you're never going to understand." I quietly say. My hands start sweating as they both start reading.

29

V ALERI

    I stare down at my shaky hands. The room is silent. Alex and Zach are sitting on either side of me, my brother on my right and Zach on my left. They're both reading the letters I left them.

Will they believe me? Will they think I'm making it all up?

I guess Alex finishes reading it first because he puts the paper down and wraps my body with his arms. He doesn't say anything, he just simply pulls me into his embrace.

"I'm so sorry, Val." He kisses my forehead and hugs me again.

It looks like Zachary came to an end as well because he stares at me over Alex's shoulder. But I can't look at him. The tears are threatening to fall down my cheeks because of how unfair it was what happened to me. I didn't deserve it. No one does.

Alex pulls away and sits back. I stare at my hands not wanting to meet their eyes. I'm ashamed of what happened to me. They're probably disgusted too.

"I'm sorry." I whisper.

"Don't be sorry, Valeri. You've done nothing wrong, okay?"

"I hurt you." I look at Zach.

"It's okay. You didn't have a choice." He pulls me onto his chest. I close my eyes and breathe in.

"I don't think I can make it." I mutter but they both hear me.

"We'll help you, okay?" Zach kisses my forehead. Then he looks up and nods at Alex.

My brother stands up to leave the room. "Where are you going?"

"I want to talk to you." Zach responds.

Its only us two now.

"You don't remember, do you?"

I sit up and curiously look at him. "Remember what?"

Context?

"How do I tell you this?" He sighs. "You had a friend when you were younger back at home. The one named Zachary."

Huh? How the hell does he know that?

Except if...

"Yeah?"

I need him to confirm it.

"He taught you how to swim." He whispers.

I can see his face clearly now. I can see a boy in it. The one I knew a few years ago.

The fuck?

ZACHARY

Valeri's arms are suddenly around my neck and her body on mine. I hug her waist and pull her closer. She sobs in my shoulder and I kiss her cheek.

"Why didn't you tell me?" She asks. Her face still buried in the crook of my neck.

"You were doing great when you came here and I didn't want to bring you back in the past." I whisper.

"Maybe none of this would happen if you told me in the beginning." She says quietly.

"I know, gorgeous, and I will regret it for the rest of my life. I wanted the best for you and I fucked up."

"It's not your fault." She sighs. "I don't blame you."

"Why did you leave?" I hear her asking.

"I had to. I'm sorry, but you know how it is with my parents. They came here because of Cade."

She sits up straight. "Cade?" Her voice shakes.

"Yeah, you already know I was adopted, but my parents had another kid a year before they got me. It was Cade. They sent him away and when he found out that they adopted me, he was really mad and jealous. He despises me now."

"I'm so sorry, sweetheart, that you had to go through everything alone and because of me." I feel tears in my eyes.

"Shhhh. It's okay. I don't blame you." She hugs me again. I breathe in her scent.

I cannot believe this is happening. I finally told her.

I was too late, though.

We sit there wrapped in each other's arms until we hear a soft knock on the door. Alex enters and sits down on the bed. Valeri is still sitting in my embrace. My best friend smiles at his sister.

VALERI

I don't know how long I stay in Zach's arms but I don't want to be anywhere else. I can't believe about him and Cade. That's why Cade did it, right? I can't blame Zach. I know he wanted the best for me but I'm really shocked.

"Valeri." I hear my brother's voice behind me.

"Mhm?" I mumble in Zach's neck.

"We need to talk about everything." He quietly says. I close my eyes shut and squeeze Zach tighter. I can't talk about it. Any of it.

"I know it's hard to talk about it, but please try. If you really won't be able to, we will wait. Or if you want to talk to someone else, you totally can." Zach is drawing circles on my back, so I almost don't hear what he says.

Okay, I can do it.

"Okay." I sit back next to Zach.

"I'll take you to the doctor tomorrow, to make sure everything is alright. Are you okay with that?"

"Yeah, I guess." I shrug with my shoulders. Honestly, I'm scared. I can't even look at my body myself and now some random person will see it.

"Do you want to press charges?" Zach asks me.

"I don't know. I don't have any proof. And the clothes that I was wearing-" I close my eyes. "He came back into my room and took them."

Zach takes my hand and starts calming me down.

"I don't know. I'll need some more time to think." I look down at my hands.

"That's okay." Alex encourages me.

I can't hold my tears anymore. They spill down my cheeks before I can stop them.

Zach pulls me against his chest. "It's okay, gorgeous."

"I'm was so scared. I'm was so so scared." I sob. "And I told them I didn't want to, but they still touched me. They weren't listening. And then he almost did it again at Madelin's. I didn't know what to do."

Zach puts my hair behind my ear and kisses my forehead.

"And I can't stop taking pills and cutting myself." I whisper. "It's been going on for years and I don't think I'll ever be able to stop."

"Do you think going to the rehab would help you?"

"I- I don't wanna go there. I want to try again here with you. If it gets worse, I'll consider it."

"I'm so proud of you, gorgeous."

I smile up at him and then at my brother.

~~~

Alex wakes me up a few hours later. "You have to eat." Hes been trying to convince me for a couple of minutes now.

"Eat, and then Zach is going to help you change the bandages." My brother continues.

I finally give in and take a bite. Alex helps me eat half of the food on the plate. He helps me up and walks me to the bathroom. I do what I have to and then Zach enters. He kisses my forehead and helps me hop on the counter.

He takes some bandages while I try to put the old one off. I suck at it.

"Let me." Zach pulls my hand away and unwraps the other one. I can't help but admire him. His dark hair and green eyes. He makes me nervous but also comfortable.

"Done." He chuckles when he notices me staring at him. "Do you want me to help you with the ones on your thighs too? If you're comfortable, of course."

"I- uhh sure."

Zach helps me pull my sweats down to my ankles and does the same as he did on my arms. I feel tension between us. We still haven't talked about us. I'm scared to start the conversation. What if he doesn't want to be with me anymore?

"Valeri." Someone touches my cheek and I'm pulled back to the reality. I must have zoned out. "Are you okay? What were you thinking about?"

I looked down at my wrapped thighs. "Do you still hate me?"

He looks shocked. "What? Hate you?" I shrug with my shoulders. "I just thought- "

A finger is put over my lips. "Shhh, I could never hate you gorgeous. It hurt me but now I know it wasn't true so it doesn't hurt anymore." He palms my cheek. I realise he came closer, so he's now standing between my legs.

Butterflies.

"You're the strongest, the most perfect person I've ever met and I'm so glad I got a chance to meet you. If I could I would take all your pain, I would go back in the past just so I could stay with you through it all." I can feel my cheeks are red.

Wow.

I stare at him stunned. No one ever told me anything like this and it kind of feels unreal.

I'm so in love with him.

His face is closer now, his lips almost touching mine, his breath on my face.

Just kiss me already-

One of his hands gently grips my hip, while the other one is still under my cheek.

"I love you too, Valeri."

Before I can process what he said, his lips are on mine.

-j

30

V ALERI

Suddenly, my hands are in Zach's hair as I kiss him. His soft lips are moving in rhythm with mine and his tongue makes its way in my mouth. I pull him closer by his shirt and kiss him with more passion.

I pull away and we both catch our breaths. "Come on, let's go to bed." He sighs.

Zach helps me put my sweats back on and then I'm lifted in the air. I wrap my legs around his waist and he brings me back to bed. He slowly tucks me in and then gets under himself.

My head is on his chest as I hug his waist. He's trailing his fingers through my hair and it's slowly making me sleepy. I listen to his heartbeat knowing I'm not alone as I drift off.

~~~

I'm woken up by the sunlight the next day. I look around and then notice Zach lying next to me.

"How'd you sleep?" He asks me.

"Alright I guess." And that's when I realise I've slept the whole night without taking pills. I really do need them now, though.

I know my brother and Zach know about everything now and they're here to support me but addiction doesn't go away that quickly.

I really need something. I feel aching on my arms and thighs.

"I will be right back. I'll just get some clothes from my room, okay?" I don't look at Zach. I'm scared he's going to see right through me.

"Do you want me to go with you?"

"You don't have to. It's okay." I reassure him and then climb over him to get to the door. When I stand up dizziness consumes my body and I have to lean my hand to the wall to keep myself up.

Zach's hands are around my waist now as he helps me to the door. We make our way to my room.

"Are you sure you want to go inside?" Zach asks me and I realise I froze.

I nod and slowly open the door. Everything is cleaned up. They must have gone through every drawer to throw away whatever they found.

I approach my wardrobe and take out some clothes. I search for anything they forgot.

"You have doctor's appointment in an hour." I hear Zach behind me. I completely forgot about that.

"Okay." That's when I notice a blade under the clothes. I slowly slide it in my pocket and then take out the clothes I picked.

"Are you done?" I nod and we go back to the room. I change in his bathroom but I don't think it's a good idea to do it now, so I hide it somewhere where Zach won't look. I'm staying in his room from now on.

After I'm done I get out and see Zach sitting on the bed. "Let's go." He takes my hand and we leave the house.

While driving he's drawing circles on the back of my hand with his fingers. He must have noticed I'm anxious.

"It'll be okay." He looks at me sideways. "What is it?"

I sigh. "I don't wanna go inside alone." I whisper but he hears me.

He stops the engine infront of a hospital. "I can go with you if you want."

"Really?"

"Of course." He smiles at me and gets out of the car. I follow him and as we're walking inside he takes my hand and softly kisses my cheek.

~~~

We're back home now. It went well and everything was fine. Zach was with me the whole time.

We walk down the hall and hear my brother cooking from the kitchen. The whole house smells of food.

"Hey, is everything okay?" Alex immediately approaches and hugs me.

"Yeah, nothing serious."

"Good, come eat now." He smiles at me.

I feel Zach's hand on my lower back as I walk to the table.

~~~

It's evening now. Zach and I are chilling in his room and Alex is out with Madelin and others. I honestly don't want to see them right now. I

understand their actions but I don't feel like I can face them anytime soon.
I'll take some time for myself.

Zach is lying on my chest as I trail my fingers down his arm, the one he's
hugging my waist with.

We still haven't talked yet. I think he's giving me time to decide when.

I don't realise I'm scratching my wrist until Zach puts his hand over mine.

"You okay?"

"Yeah." I want to get better I really do but I can't just switch. My mind is
filled with thoughts of relapsing. I've been clean for two days and I really
need a release.

"You're not. Come here." He lies down on his back and pulls me closer so
my head is now resting on his chest.

"Do you want to talk about it?" He asks.

"I don't know." I mumble.

"Take your time. Tell me when you're ready."

"Okay."

We stay like that for some time until I start becoming sleepy. I decide I
should change and then come back to bed.

I slowly sit up and take some clothes and then shut myself in the bathroom.

I change into a crop top because it's too hot in here. I ignore the healing
scars on my arms. Then I take off my sweats and look at myself. I don't
want to relapse but I really really need it right now, so I do it quickly. I
don't go deep, just a tiny cut.

After that, I wrap it and put on my shorts.

When I'm done, I go back to Zach's room. He's lying on his bed staring at me. I feel exposed. My scars are exposed and I try to cover them by wrapping my wrms around my waist. I quickly approach the bed and Zach sits up.

"What took you so long?" He asks as he unwraps my arms looking down at my body. I'm standing between his legs and he's making me nervous.

I shrug with my shoulders and look down at him.

He hugs my waist still sitting down as I'm standing. "You're so beautiful." He mutters.

I smile because I don't think I was supposed to hear that since he said it so quietly as if he was talking to himself.

"Zach?"

"Mhm?"

"I'm curious about something. About Cade." I want to throw up when I say his name.

Zachary helps me back on bed so I'm sitting on his lap and he's leaning back on the headboard.

"What about him?" His voice is low and full of hate and rage.

"He said that he was doing it all to hurt you. I don't get it. Have something happened between you two?"

He tenses and stays quiet as if he's thinking about something.

"Yes. I don't know why I haven't told you this yet but..." he stops. "...Cade is my biological brother."

Did I miss a chapter?

"What?"

"I didn't know for quite some time. You know I was adopted. We were both in foster care and I was adopted first, but my parents didn't want two children. We moved a lot so one was enough. Cade... he was adopted years later by a family that didn't care about him. He wasn't treated right his whole childhood. When I moved here, I saw him again for the first time in years. He knew who I was and he knew how good my childhood was. He was jealous. He still is. I knew he wanted to hurt me but I never imagined he would use you to do it. I'm so sorry, Valeri. I'm so sorry you were the one to get hurt in the end."

I'm in shock. Really, my body is frozen and I don't know what to think or do.

"Why didn't you tell me you had a brother?" I ask.

"I considered telling you about him a lot of times but I wasn't ready. I don't know." Zach strokes my thigh while he's reading my expression.

"Isn't he Madelin's cousin?"

"Yes, her aunt and uncle were the ones to adopt him."

"Does she know that? Does anyone other know?" I ask.

Zach shakes with his head. "No, except for Alex no one knows Cade was adopted. Madelin was too young to remember it."

"I- I don't know what to say." I let out a laugh that quickly dies down. I'm in shock.

"I'll blame myself forever because of him hurting you. I'm sorry Valeri, gorgeous, I'm sorry for everything."

I lean my forehead on his. "It's not your fault. You didn't do anything wrong." I whisper.

I realise his cheeks are wet because of his tears and I quickly wipe them with my thumbs. "He hurt you. He hurt you to the point you tried to... tried to... you know what."

"But it wasn't your fault. I love you, Zach. I don't blame you for what happened. You mean so much to me." I kiss his forehead.

"I really wanna be with you again." He whispers.

"I want to be with you too." I smile at him.

He looks unsure as if I'm lying, so I put my lips on his and kiss him.

THE END

Milton Keynes UK
Ingram Content Group UK Ltd.
UKHW031839121024
449535UK00010B/628